VISION

Unlocking the Secrets to
Optimizing Your Natural, Mental,
and Spiritual Eyesight

MICHAEL S. NIMMONS

authorHOUSE®

AuthorHouse™
1663 Liberty Drive
Bloomington, IN 47403
www.authorhouse.com
Phone: 1 (800) 839-8640

Published by AuthorHouse   01/17/2018

ISBN: 978-1-5462-2242-2 (sc)
ISBN: 978-1-5462-2494-5 (e)

Library of Congress Control Number: 2018900182

Print information available on the last page.

All bible scripture taken from KJV

CONTENTS

"We didn't come here to fear the future, we came here to shape it." - **President Barack Obama,** 44th President of the United States

DEDICATION

This book is dedicated to my beautiful wife Tiffany Nimmons and my three lovely children; Stephen-Michael, Mya Grace, and Lauren Michele. They are my heartbeat, they are the reason that I live and breathe. Each of them have a unique quality that makes them so very special to me. I love them so much and could not imagine my world without them.

Tiffany, you are the love of my life and I truly appreciate all that you are to this family. I love your warmth, your encouragement and your enduring support for our every endeavor. I wish you much success in your all of your dreams and your desires. I hope that I have inspired you as you certainly have inspired me.

Stephen, you are such a bright and intelligent young man. You remind me of myself when I was your age. I wish nothing but the best for you and your future endeavors.

Mya, you are such a sweet and talented young lady. You make me smile every time I see you jumping and flipping around the house, because I know we've got a future Olympian on our hands. Just don't break the furniture.

Lauren, you are a born leader. I see the leader in you come out every day you're telling your older brother and sister what to do. I know you have a bright future ahead of you and I can't wait to see what God has in store for you.

ABOUT THE AUTHOR

As President and CEO of Michael Nimmons Ministries, Inc., and Executive Director of "The Vision Initiative:" a non-profit organization designed to give young people a new vision of themselves, Pastor Nimmons is a dynamic and anointed servant of God, endeavoring to take the message of the gospel to the world. Author of "Who Told You That You Were Naked;" his first book which sold nearly one thousand copies, Pastor Nimmons in his new book entitled "*Vision*," is continuing to make his mark as an up and coming author. He is also a radio show host of the "Thinking Out Loud" Radio Show, which is a weekly talk show where news, politics and current events are the centerpiece of discussion. You can listen to his show each week "LIVE" on Blog Talk Radio (http://www. blogtalkradio.com/thinkingoutloudradio) Tuesday evenings from 8 to 9pm. The podcast can also be found on iTunes, Google Play Music and TuneIn.

A man passionate about reaching God's people through the various gifts and talents God has placed in his hands to use, Pastor Nimmons is an extraordinarily gifted and talented vessel of God. He is also an accomplished speaker, who has won numerous awards for oratory as well as possesses an impressive repertoire of speaking engagements. He enjoys preaching in the pulpit as well teaching and motivating people wherever he can.

He also currently serves as Vice-Chairman of the Council of Pastors (C.O.P.) of Greater Grace Temple (GGT); where he a is an Assistant Pastor to Bishop Charles H. Ellis III; Presiding Bishop of the Pentecostal Assemblies of the World, Inc. Former Youth Pastor of GGT where he served faithfully for over 4yrs, Pastor Nimmons dutifully puts forth his best efforts to whatever God has placed in his hands to do. Working diligently in the vineyard as both a preacher and teacher, he loves sharing the Word of God with everyone he comes in contact with.

A father and a husband, Pastor Nimmons understands the importance of family. He is the husband to beautiful wife Tiffany, father to three lovely children Stephen-Michael, Maya Grace and Lauren Michelle. Nurturing and supporting healthy family relationships is one of his keys to being an effective minister.

An author, writer, radio show host and blogger, you can find Pastor Nimmons all over the World Wide Web. Friend him on Facebook, follow him on Twitter @

TOLRadioShowHostMSN and watch him on Youtube all from his personal ministry site www.MichaelNimmons.org..

Writer, entrepreneur, preacher, teacher, and motivational speaker; Pastor Nimmons is poised to become one of the leading voices of his generation.

To find out how to book Pastor Nimmons for your next event or to get more information about Michael Nimmons Ministries, Inc., visit www.MichaelNimmons.org.

INTRODUCTION

How do you discuss a topic as broad and as bold as vision? How do you begin unpacking the many layers of a voluminous topic such as vision and make it relatable and palatable to everyone who reads this book? This is what is the exciting part about writing this book, because it is filled with insightful and motivational components that will help you move from one level to the next. I guarantee reading this book will be a thrill ride; a journey worth taking, because as you read you will be empowered, as you read you be motivated, as you read you will be inspired and challenged to do the unimaginable. The God-given insights in this book will help you see yourself fulfilling your purpose and realizing your untapped potential.

In this book, we are also a bit autobiographical, in that we share how vision has impacted our lives, we share some hidden gems from our family as well as share some past experiences that we believe will help you to jumpstart your vision. We are also a bit biographical as well. In this book, we discuss the likes of men and women such as Dr. Martin Luther King Jr. Helen Keller and World Leader, Apartheid survivor and South Africa's 1st African President – Nelson

Mandela. Who from his prison cell at Robbins Island of 27yrs not only envisioned a free South Africa but strategized on how to make his vision a reality. And, once freed hit the ground running, planning, working and organizing to achieve the goal of freeing South Africa from the treacherous bands of Apartheid. His ascension to South Africa's highest office as not only the nation's 1st African President, but democratically elected President Nelson Mandela's example should clearly demonstrate to us that we must be about the business of actively pursuing our dreams and visions. He truly is one of history's greatest revolutionaries. We can ill-afford to let any more time pass while our visions lie dormant and become nothing more than cannon fodder for the enemy. In this book, we plan to discuss the topic of vision from three separate vantage points; naturally, mentally and spiritually. Three perspectives that offer us very different insights into this very important word.

Vision in the broad context of its understanding is basically having a goal or idea of a direction or path you would like to pursue for yourself. From a practical standpoint, vision; naturally speaking, is simply what you can physically see in front of you. Our natural eyes are the window into our souls; this is an old saying in American culture that suggest that our eyes are the windows into our deepest and innermost thoughts. What we naturally see has a certain way of effecting or impacting us, and how is it that two people can see the same thing and both walk away with two different perceptions of what they saw? Natural sight is so important, because by it we are able to appreciate the world around us through the natural eyes that God has given us, which is an tremendously precious gift. There are a number of people on this planet that do not have the gift of sight, they are naturally blind and cannot see the world around them. Their blindness does not make them any less of a person, it means that they have to use their other remaining senses to appreciate the world around them. When one says, they have a vision, it typically means that can see in their mind's eye a vision for themselves that will happen or unfold for the future. This is not necessarily a God-given vision, but it can be simply a general view of one's life and the direction it is headed in. And, finally there is spiritual vision that only comes from God. This is the kind of vision that God provides with which offers us a window into our purpose and helps us to answer the questions, why am I here? Every man, woman, boy and girl was created with purpose, by purpose, on purpose and it's our life's duty to find out what that purpose is. And, it makes all the sense in the world to seek direction from our Creator, who has the details of our life already meted out. Who better to ask what our purpose is than the one who is solely responsible for our existence, if anyone knows He definitely should. What's unfortunate is that some people spend their whole lives seeking out the wrong person to find their purpose. Instead of seeking out the Creator we seek guidance from His other creations, which results in a sordid whirlwind of confusion and ultimately ends in us having more questions than we have answers.

As we discuss the secrets to optimize your natural, mental and spiritual eyesight in this book, I believe it is important to note that all three works interdependently of one another in helping us to understand the scope of what it is we are seeing. Our natural sight, helps us to process what we see around us; it helps us to answer the questions of who, what, when and where. Our natural sight is integral in allowing us to internalize our surroundings. Although, we know that people are still able to function without having their natural sight. In fact, the absence of natural sight heightens their other 5 senses in ways that help them to internalize their surroundings without being able to physically see what is around them. The beauty of the world that God created is prima facia evidence that we are not here by accident or by coincidence, but we are here because of a power much greater than ours. Natural eyesight is not the focus of the book, we are not spending time conducting an examination of a person's natural eyesight from a medical standpoint. Natural eyesight comes into play because it is the initial path to both mental and spiritual perception. It is according to Luke 11:34 (NKJV) that natural eyes are considered the light of the body, "…therefore when your eye is good, your whole body is full of light. But when your eye is bad, then your whole body is full of darkness." We are impacted negatively and positively by what we see. This is why we have to strive to protect our eye gates, because they are indeed the window into our soul. Likewise, it is our mental and spiritual perception that ultimately determines how we will respond to what we naturally see. So, we will not be spending time providing tips on how to take care of your physical eyesight per see, because this is not the purpose ofr this book. However, natural eyesight is essentially the gateway to our mental and spiritual eyesight, so it is very important that we guard our natural eye gates as they are our first line of sight that helps us to determine our collective response in to how we see the world around us.

Natural sight also works interdependently with our mental sight, because what we see naturally must be processed mentally as well. It is our mind that ultimately tell us what we are seeing naturally. While this might seem like a fairly simplistic realization, in the context of this book, we will see how our mind can work for or against us when it comes to processing what we see naturally. Many times, it is our minds eye that helps to shape a reality that exists beyond what see naturally. This is why we have some people who consider themselves optimists, and others who consider themselves pessimists. Inasmuch as they have consciously chosen to take opposite ends of the spectrum when it comes to examining the same reality naturally. The optimist says the proverbial glass is "half full" and the pessimists says the proverbial glass is "half empty" Now they are both looking at the same glass, with the same amount of liquid, but each person decided to take the opposing view of the other based on how they mentally perceived the reality they naturally saw. Why is that? Why didn't they both see the glass the same way? There are several contributing factors that determine why each person decided to look at the same glass differently, and we endeavor to examine these factors as we journey through the chapters of this book together.

Spiritual eyesight or vision; in my humble opinion, trumps the other two because it can create an alternate reality outside of what we might see naturally that lends itself to more divine origins. These divine origins supersede any physical or mental evidence that we may have been seen or perceived. When vision is looked at from this perspective it is thoroughly divine and governed primarily by a higher power that uses this type of vision to show us a glimpse of our true selves. Spiritual eyesight or insight; depending on how you look at it, sets aside any natural or even mental evidence that might cause one to think negatively or pessimistically about any situation or circumstance. And, because of its divine origins when one is truly dialed into their spiritual eyesight, anything is truly possible.

In this book, we will discuss in great detail the dynamics of each of these three paradigms of vision and how they function and work interdependently of one another. What is interesting is how our lives are ultimately shaped by whatever facet of vision that we've allowed to have preeminence in our lives. Hopefully, at the end of this journey you will discover who you are, and more importantly if you are satisfied with being who are you or have you found a better visual path to enriching your life.

Some people are very practical or realistic when it comes to looking at life and looking at themselves. They've taken into account all of the natural evidence regarding their lives and use this evidence to help them govern their life's decisions. They've chosen to take a more practical or pragmatic approach to living. It is usually these people whose lives are shaped primarily by what they see around them; their environment, their neighborhoods, schools, church, etc.

All three of these facets of vision determines how we see the world, how we see each other, how we see ourselves and even our how we see our Creator. Journey with us through this book as we navigate through this process of understanding vision from a natural, mental and spiritual perspective. Each has its own specific purpose, but each one heavily influences the other. Not one facet of vision is independent of the other, but they all work interdependently and can either help us or hinder us from reaching our goals. It is important that we understand the importance and significance of each facet and how they help us to understand and appreciate life, the world around us and even our purpose.

The key in all of these is to keep God at the center, because when He is at the center no matter what we physically see or mentally perceive, our spirit will remind us that God is in ultimate control our lives. Whenever we allow our spirit to guide both our mind and our body every facet of vision will be completely in sync with one another. Regardless if what we see is contrary to what we believe or see spiritually, our natural and mental eyesight will be influenced by our spiritual eyesight. The same with our perceptual or mental vision, our spirit will undergird our mind to only yield positive reinforcement at times when we what we see is contrary to what our spirit is telling us is there.

Vision; how what we see ultimately determines what we do. All three of these diverse visual paradigms help us determine our course of action. Whatever dimension of vision is most important to you will ultimately determine your perception, your behavior and most importantly your response. How we respond to any crisis is based upon our perception of what we see. For some; the physical and mental dimensions of vision are the two that are used to form a perception of what we see. Our natural sight is used to physically assess the crisis that requires our response, and our mental sight is called upon to determine our mental health as it relates to what we naturally see.

The goal of the book is once the reader has finished, they will look at themselves and their lives completely different. They will encounter a mental and spiritual awakening that will hopefully begin to impact them naturally as well. The reader will see themselves and their potential much differently than they ever did before. They will also see things about their life a bit clearer and with a greater understanding of what their purpose is in life. Clear sight equates to a clear understanding of my purpose. My vision only gets blurry when there is confusion about what it is I was put on this earth to accomplish. We want to equip the reader with natural, mental as well as spiritual techniques to seeing clearer and thinking more positively about themselves, their lives and their purpose. It all begins with what you see, and how you ultimately interpret what you see.

The final very important component of this book is it's call to action. In the final pages of this book it is our desire to motivate and inspire you to pursue whatever dream or vision that you believed you've been divinely assigned. It would be a complete and utter travesty for you to spend time reading this book only to put it down or to put it back on the shelf as just another part of your literary collection. But, I want to challenge you to actively engage your own vision; this book is a reminder to some and an introduction to many others of their God-given purpose and what they should be spending their life trying to accomplish.

Below are some practical ways that you can start to engage your own vision, and begin to optimize the mental perception of yourself. In this book, we endeavor to give spiritual as well as practical examples that you can use in your everyday life. We want this book to be effective in both the pulpit and the corporate boardroom, the executive suite to the domestic homemaker. Below are just a few of the natural, mental and spiritual examples that we will discuss throughout the book.

Internalize what you see with a grain of salt; its not always how it looks

- Don't get caught up in what you see naturally. Our natural sight is not the end but many times it is the building blocks to real vision.

Do things naturally to raise your level of self-awareness

- Dress for success, hang around positive people, immerse yourself into positive thinking, read books that empower you to think positively

Don't be afraid to step outside of your comfort zone;

- You have to expose yourself to the greatness that you want to achieve. You cannot achieve what you haven't seen or haven't been exposed to. Exposure opens up your mind to what is possible, and it begins in large part by what you see

Talk to yourself;

- You have to encourage yourself; self-motivate. You are not always going to be surrounded by positive influences, so in some cases you are going to have to be your own cheerleader. Don't be afraid to pat your own self on the back

Create Vision Boards

- In our last chapter, we go into detail about some of real ways you can mobilize your vision and vision boards are a big part of that. You have to be able to see your vision in written form so you can begin to mete out the nuts and bolts of it. You have to be able to see it before you can see it.

These are just a few of the practical examples that we plan to discuss in this book that are also proven methods of visual exploration that have been employed by many successful people. If you are stuck in a rut this, book is for you, if you are looking for ways to mobilize your vision this book is for you, if you know there is a greater purpose for your existence, this book is for you, if you are relying too heavily on what you see with your natural eyes, this book is for you, if you need a good kick in the pants before you get started seriously pursuing your vision, THIS BOOK IS FOR YOU!!!

CHAPTER 1

THE PURPOSE OF VISION

Vision is the Source and Hope of life. The greatest gift ever given to mankind was not the gift of sight, but the gift of vision. Sight is a function of the eyes; vision is a function of the heart. Eyes that look are common, but eyes that see are rare. Nothing noble or noteworthy was ever done on earth without vision.

—*Myles Munroe*

This quote from Dr. Myles Munroe is so powerful and profound that it encapsulates in just a few sentences the tremendous purpose that vision itself contains. Dr. Munroe first points out the distinction between sight and vision. The former deals only with the natural and how one can physically see the world around them. However, the latter points to one's ability to see through the physical into the metaphysical and ethereal to a place where our purpose is divinely defined.

Dr. Munroe contends that "vision is the source and hope of life." Herein lies the fundamental purpose of vision: it is the substrata of life and the origin of life or what life is made of. It divinely reaffirms the genesis of humanity through the lens of purpose, which also happens to be the companion of vision.

Intermingled throughout this revelation of vision and purpose is the confirmation that life is not coincidental; life is not arbitrary or accidental, but is filled with purpose. We can see purpose intertwined into everything that was ever created, just as Dr. Munroe stated: "There is nothing noble or noteworthy [that] was ever done on earth without vision."

When you step back and reflect upon the magnificence of the world that God created, you cannot help but imagine the forethought and vision that must have gone into the creation of not just the world but the entire universe. Vision is the centerpiece of the earth's design. You can see the harmony and unity in the solar system. You can see the economy of the planets and the distance they are from each other and how they could not exist by accident, but must have been brought about by someone's divine design. Vision from this standpoint is a blueprint or a layout that reflects the mind of the Creator.

From this vantage point vision as a blueprint, you see organization; you see harmony; you see-uniformity; you see that there was a clear plan put in place even before anything was created. The existence of a blueprint refutes the notion of evolution completely because a blueprint or a plan speaks to intention, and intention speaks to purpose.

So the question then becomes: whose plan was it? When you have the answer, you also have the answer to a host of other questions which are directly or indirectly related.

The existence of Earth and its neighboring planets also speaks to the vision and purpose it represents. Men and women have speculated for years regarding the earth's existence, and none have been able to offer a sufficient alternative to the genesis of human beings through creation. Absent from every theory, every hypothesis, every argument ever formulated is the very same word that is the undergirding of our human existence: purpose. We are not here on this massive ball of gasses orbiting around with other planets for absolutely no reason. Furthermore, the harmony and symmetry that exists in not just the Earth but in the entire universe speaks to a much greater and larger purpose than we even realize.

The Five Ws

The problem with science is it can almost always tell us what but cannot always tell us why. And in a real sense, science is essentially God's stenographer, feverishly recording the facts of everything that God created but never able to really tell us why, nor give credit where it really belongs.

It tells us what satisfies only part of our sensibilities and curiosities, but at the end of the day, we really want to know why. There is no man-made theories or hypothesis that even comes close to explaining the existence of the universe without purpose. Without purpose, we are just a bunch of evolutionary creatures cohabiting on a planet that we know very little about. Without purpose, the big bang theory would be spot-on: we are a product of a seismic atmospheric explosion that began a series of events ultimately leading to the culmination of humankind.

The interesting part about this is that I choose to believe in the genesis of humans through creation, not because it answers the question of why, but because it also answers the question of who. Knowing who is responsible is just as important as knowing why it happened, because the revelation of the who would have to be just as compelling as the answer why. Who stepped out on nothing and said, "Let there be"—and there was? Who made the sun, the moon, and the stars? Who made the animals? Who made the planets? Who made the geography and topography of planet Earth?

It would seem that asking the question who also begins to answer the question of why, because the splendor of creation is a mere reflection of its creator. The magnificence of creation ultimately speaks to the magnitude of its Creator. The Creator would have to be greater than what He created because His greatness is reflected in what He created. Just as Michelangelo painted the *Mona Lisa* or the Sistine Chapel, which are monuments to his greatness as an artist, likewise the world and everything in it reflects the greatness of God that science continues to assert doesn't exist. This is also why He is noticeably absent from their theories about the universe. When you remove God from anything, it automatically loses its purpose. Thus removing God from the arcane theories of science only makes their result achievements inconsequential and arbitrary.

Our lives are a microcosmic representation of the macrocosmic genius of the Creator who spoke the world into existence with the power of His voice. Just as this omniscient God collaborated with His own mind and word to create the entire universe, our individual lives, undergirded by purpose, are orchestrated and guided by purpose. There was nothing done in the beginning, middle, or even the end that purpose was not

, is no and will not intricately involved with. Purpose is the driving force behind everything in the world in which we live, although some would have you believe that the origin of our existence is merely coincidental, a result of some cosmic explosion that eventually concluded with the phenomenon of evolution, which science alone can explain.

However, as we look at the magnificent world in which we live, we cannot help but see purpose reflected in everything that was created. It is hard to comprehend the world according to the narrow-minded musings of science, which explains the earth's existence as purely coincidental, with no one or nothing solely responsible for the earth's existence except an explosion that set evolution into motion.

But if evolution is the nucleus of our existence, if evolution is the architect of the world in which we live, then who or what is responsible for evolution? Who decided to use evolution as the instrument to create something that never was? Where did the idea come from? These are all valid questions, but questions for which Charles Darwin's *Theory of Evolution* does not have concrete answers.

The centerpiece of Darwin's theory is that time ultimately led us to the place we are today. But time cannot explain the harmony that exists in nature. Time cannot explain the existence of a solar system with planets that systematically orbit without ever colliding with one another. Time cannot explain the life-giving energy of the sun and how, in spite of its tremendous distance from the Earth, it continues to facilitate the intricacies of weather around the world.

Time cannot answer these questions, but purpose certainly can. Purpose picks up where time conveniently leaves off and offers us a complete and intelligent explanation of the genesis of humanity and rightfully attributes the creation of the world to its author and creator, God.

It is important to understand that those who believe in the genesis of creation do so not just because they believe in a Supreme Being, but because they believe in a Supreme Being who created the world and everything in it and is also accompanied by purpose. Purpose helps to makes sense of a God who most times does not make sense. And that should not make Him less believable, but it speaks directly to the divine nature of His character, which He boldly professes of Himself: in Isaiah 55:8(KJV) God's truest character is revealed;

> *"My ways are not your ways and my thoughts are not your thoughts. For as high as the heaven is from the earth, so are my thoughts from your thoughts."*

For some, this is a hard scripture to digest because it is natural for us to need to understand and comprehend everything. And when we can't seem to understand or comprehend something, it's harder for us to believe in its existence. Hence the challenge that comes with believing in a God that you cannot see or touch.

What's even more ironic about this discussion of the existence of God is that He is the one who gave us these senses that we use to analyze and dissect everything. And yet we can't use any of these senses to comprehend or understand the God who gave them to us. What turns this argument on its head is considering the magnificence of a God who would give us the senses to comprehend and understand everything but Him and still allow us to experience His presence on another spiritual plateau—if only we are willing to relinquish the propensity to comprehend Him through our five senses and to simply believe that He exists. Our belief or non-belief does not in any way help or hurt Him. It works to our benefit or ultimate demise, as the Apostle Paul declares in Hebrews 11:5(KJV): "For without faith it is impossible to please the Lord, for he that cometh to God must believe that He is and that He is a Rewarder of them that diligently seek Him." So it is in our best interest to believe in Him and not the other way around.

The Road Less Traveled

The Bible says in Proverbs 28:15, "where this is no vision the people perish." In other words, death accompanies a people with no vision. Lewis Carroll said, " …if you don't know where you are going, any road will take you there." In this quote, we see the importance of having some direction, because any road cannot take you where you need to go. You cannot venture down any road and be successful, you cannot journey down any road and find your destination. Any road isn't sufficient in determining the right path to take literally or figuratively. So, in these quotes we see the importance of having a vision and not vision in the sense of physical sight. We are not referring to a person's inability to physically see, which will ultimately determine their success or failure. But, having a sense of purpose and direction in one's life that will eventually lead them to where they were divinely destined to be. When you examine the scripture from Proverbs 29:18(KJV) that asserts, "where there is no vision the people perish," there is no truer statement that can be uttered. We see this happening and transpiring across the country, young people with no sense of direction, no guidance, and no sense of purpose; involved in all types of foolishness that ultimately leads them nowhere.

Looking at the behavior of some of today's youth and the trends that become popular through social media and other outlets, just when you think you have seen it all they always find a way to shock and surprise you all over again. Watching the evening newscast, you see and hear some of the most disturbing news surrounding our young people, primarily because they are a people operating without a vision. One of the most disturbing parts about most of the violent crimes that take place that could easily be avoided, but I believe is symptomatic of people without direction, is the time of day or night that they take place. 1, 2, 3, 4 o'clock in the morning, a young girl is raped and murdered, a young boy is shot at a gas station in cold blood. I was always taught as a child that nothing good happens in the streets at night. That's why my parents use to always tell us when we were kids, "you better be home before the streets lights came on." This was when we were of some age and we could go outside without parental supervision. At the time, I thought it was unfair to have to sometimes stop in the middle of a pick-up basketball game or football game, because the street lights came on and have got to go home. The unmitigated gall of my parents to make that a rule in our house for us to be home before the street lights came on was blatantly unfair and egregious. And, most times when I left I would be one of the few that had to leave, because of the unfair edict that I had to obey if I planned to continue living at my parent's house. However, as an adult as I look back on what I thought was an unfair rule, I now see the rationale and the immense value associated with it. This rule came from a home where there were some expectations that were put in place for the occupants of that residence. I came from a home where any effort I gave was not acceptable; I came from a home where there is a right and a wrong way of doing things; I came from a home where respect was both earned and given. And, it was those values that I was raised upon as a child that has allowed me to survive well into my adulthood. I use the word "survive" because nowadays; it seems, that the advice "we" were given as children are the "Survival Tips" that kids today need for "them" to see "their" grandkids. And now I can see the immense benefits of obeying my parent's egregious rules and regulations, because now I'm old enough to not only appreciate their value, but to turnaround and instill them into the children God has gifted me to raise. What is also true of the rules that came from my unreasonable parents is those rules were a direct indication of some very different expectations they had for my life than the parents of some of the other kids in my neighborhood. Those expectations originated from a place of vision they had in mind for me even before I could even see it myself. The path that was chosen for the children that lived in our house did not at all mean that the parents / guardians of the other neighbor kids did not want the best for them as well. What it meant was that each of them had different ideas on what they thought was best as well as how to ultimately achieve that goal. One thing is very true out of all of the home training the children of our house received, children with vision almost always come from parents with vision.

Worth and Work

We often steer clear of anything that requires work, this is the "I want my cake and eat it too" kind of generation. No one wants to have anything to do with work or associated at all with the term. However, I was always taught that anything worth having you are going to work to get it. Two words that contain so much meaning and significance; "worth" and "work." "If it's worth it then I'm going to work for it, and if I have to work for it then it must be worth it." This is probably the thought process of 100% of this world's population. I personally do not like to waste time. I don't like wasting other people's time and I certainly don't want other people to waste my time. Why, because I realize the value of time and because the value of time is closely related to purpose. We are not given time to waste, but we were given time to produce. God wants to see our value of time reflected in how we spend it. The worth of God's vision should be reflected in the work that it takes to bring it to pass. Conversely, the work of God's vision is reflective of it's worth or its value. God never gives us anything that is worthless. He never associates Himself with anything worthless. Our worth is directly tied to the work that God put into bringing us to the place we are today. The worth and the work are symmetrically tied together, because one helps to support the other.

Going back to our earlier example of our parental influences, even before we knew God had a vision in mind for us, we knew that our parents did. And, we were constantly reminded of this every time they had some "work" for us to do because there was definitely some "worth" associated with it both in the short run as well as the long run. The immediate worth of the work originated from our parents request to do the work. We understand that their words had value, their request should be honored because they are our parents and should be respected. We consented to do what they asked because we lived in their house under their roof and reaped the benefits of their provision by virtue of the blood running through our veins.

The long run of the worth of the work that my parents requested us to do was the lesson of responsibility. Responsibility is an important virtue that good parents teach their children, because the posterity of their offspring is hinged upon not just the responsibility of the parents but the responsibility of their children to the next generation. These values must be taught and instilled into our youth and on a larger scale the posterity of our society rests on the proficiency of this exchange. Essentially, what this really boils down to is that our parents saw something in us before we saw it in ourselves, and in order for them to cultivate what it was they saw they felt it was necessary to incorporate work into the daily regimen of our development. This was done to ensure that what their insight showed them will eventually materialize before their very eyes.

Eyesight vs Insight

Eyesight answers the question "what," insight answers the question "why?" You can have sight but still not be able to see, how is that even possible? But, isn't the physical act of "seeing" the manifestation or the evidence of sight? Not so, they are both operating under two completely different objectives. Dr. Munroe eluded to this in our earlier quote that sight is a function of the eyes and vision is a function of the heart. This is not a knock against your natural eyesight, because that is a very important physical attribute to have. No one volunteers to be blind, everyone wants to have their eyesight; to visually digest the magnificent landscape of the world around us is truly a gift from God. I cannot imagine not having the ability to visually appreciate the world's splendor. Eyesight is almost something we tend to take for granted until it is taken away from us. Like most things that are taken away; that we once had, a greater appreciation for it is forged. You long for it, you dread not having it. And, what about those who were blind from birth; people who never had the opportunity to see their relatives and loved ones, people who never saw the wildlife or other animals in the zoo, people who never experienced what it was like to see their reflection in the mirror, this has to be a very frustrating existence. Not knowing what anything or anyone ever looked like, this has to be a very difficult reality to accept. Yet we have people every day living without the benefit of natural sight, but they are surviving and even thriving in ways they were told they would not or could not. Modern technology has helped the blind to live in a world they cannot physically see. Brail, voice-activated devices, along with other modern conveyances that were developed to help the blind live in a world they cannot see. One amazing fact about blindness is the absence of this sixth sense heightens one of the other senses that we have. So, although a person cannot see, there hearing maybe exponentially better to compensate for the absence of sight. God has a unique way of equipping us for this journey called life even when we may not have all of the standard issued equipment when we begin.

As important as eyesight maybe in appreciating life, I would argue that insight is even more important for a person to be successful in life. Insight is what Dr. Munroe calls "seeing" which is a function of the heart. Webster defines insight as "the act or the result of apprehending the inner nature of things or seeing intuitively." Another definition says, "it is the power or the act of seeing into a situation." In other words, insight is the ability to see past what can be seen to what cannot be seen. What cannot be seen by everyone is the rarity of insight that makes it such an exclusive component of living that Dr. Munroe called it a "gift from God." Sight is one thing, but seeing is something entirely different. Everybody has sight but everybody can't see. This is what separates the real from the counterfeit, because sight only allows you to view things from the surface. It only gives you the ability to visualize things as they are, but insight allows you to go deeper, it gives you the ability to see past the surface. This is certainly rarified air, because everybody can't see past the surface; insight transcends the natural limitations that comes with sight. Insight is synonymous with true vision, because vision is what you have when you can see potential when others see poverty, you can see triumph when others only see tragedy. It really is rare when you two people can look at the same situation and because one is looking with eyesight they see disappointment, but the other person is seeing with insight and they see opportunity. With insight, you can see hope in what appears to be hopeless, you can see promise even in the midst of poverty, you can see potential when everyone else sees problems. From this vantage point, success is not limited to what you see, it is actually contingent upon what you can't see. Potential is not made up of what you see, but it is actually made up of what you can't see.

We tend to value things according to how we see them with our eyes. Our eyes give us the ability to make judgements about something even before we are able to use any of the other senses to evaluate what we see. With this in mind, we often times equate what we see higher than that which we don't see, primarily because we don't see it. However, there a lot of things that exists, but we have never seen. The wind exists, but the only proof of its existence is the feeling we get from a cool breeze from its tenacious gusts or from the view of the aftermath of the wreckage it left behind it's violent path. What we see with our eyes can easily deceive us, but what we see with our hearts can be extremely revealing.

What God Sees When He Looks at Us

To properly understand "Vision," it is God's expression of our purpose in a visible way. Sometime this takes place subconsciously or when we're asleep and sometimes it takes place when we're wide awake and completely conscious. There was an enormous amount of potential deposited in us when we were created. Great thought and deliberation was taken when considering each one of our lives before we were even a twinkle in our mother's eye.

What's interesting about vision is that it is accompanied by purpose, vision is the expression of purpose and purpose is the fulfillment of vision. The two works well together, because one is motivating and influencing the actions of the other. Vision is the handiwork of purpose, when God gifted us with a vision he also gave us purpose which directly coincides with the vision He already gave us. Our vision and purpose should work in concert with one another, you will never have a vision that your purpose will not be able to fulfill. In the same way, God will never expect you to do something that He has not already equipped you to accomplish. In other words, vision is the expectation that God has for the purpose He gave you. God will never give you something that you are not supposed to have or do anything with. So, if you have it then God gave it to you, and if He gave it to you then you are supposed to do something with it. It is quite simple, when you think about it, but we complicate things when we think about our capabilities relative to whatever vision and purpose that God has given to us to fulfill. Yes, you will feel inadequate, you will probably feel like the vision is far too big for you. These are all very realistic expressions that follow the revelation of your vision and purpose. However, that is not for you to use as an excuse not to pursue them. God's vision will always be much bigger than our vision, and the vision that He gives us will always seem bigger and more expansive than what we can handle. Just remember if He gave it you, then He's going to help you to not only see it as something that is possible, but help you to bring it to pass. If your vision is not keeping you up at night, if it doesn't cause you to spend every waking moment thinking about it, then it just might not be big enough.

God's Magnum Opus

The thesis of this chapter is simple, Great God + Great Purpose = Great Expectations. In essence, it took a great God to create a great purpose for you, which in turn produces great expectations. You see everything He creates automatically becomes a reflection of Him. There is no way for us to be His children and we not be great. The Apostle Peter in 1 Peter 2:9,

"Ye are a Chosen Generation, a Royal Priesthood and a Holy Nation. A peculiar people that he should show forth the praises of Him who brought you out of darkness into this marvelous light"

Here we can clearly see that we were intended to be a reflection of our Creator. But, with that distinction comes some great expectations. We have already established that nothing that God created was created by accident or by happenstance. And, if our existence is intentional and we know from whose intent we exist then it behooves us to get to know Him, because the closer you to get to Him the closer you get to your purpose. And the closer you get to your purpose the closer you get to meeting the great expectations that have already been set for you. By virtue of the greatness of this enterprise we called the universe, we have to believe that God didn't do all of that for us to amount to nothing. He made the investment into us so that we can bring forth tremendous fruit. In fact, His first commandment to mankind was to "be fruitful and multiply ..." I believe this commandment did not just pertain to man physical responsibility to procreate and to grow the Earth, but I believe that it directly pertains to God's general expectations for man to be productive. God say, "Here I gave you this gift, now what are you going to do with it?" Everything that we touch as His children is supposed to turn to gold. If the universe and everything in it is God's Magnum Opus then we are His Masterpieces that reflect the genius and brilliance of its Creator. We have to ask ourselves, is my life a reflection of the greatness of my Creator, am I doing all that I can to adequately reflect who it is that created me? Or is there more that I need to do to accurately reflect the brilliance of my Creator? Very pointed questions that each will have to ask ourselves as we seek out our purpose. You will find that our purpose is rightly aligned with the one who created us, which instinctively causes us to then ask, "why we're we created," inasmuch the only one who truly knows would be our Creator. Which really simplifies our quest to find our purpose, because the closer you get to your Creator the closer you get to your purpose. No one else knows more about you than the one responsible for our existence, and we tend to seek out everyone but our Creator for the merits of our purpose when they are no more responsible for our existence than we are. So, the quest or the question becomes not just knowing what to ask but who to ask. As we stated earlier the "who" is just as important as the "why."

Our Pursuit of Purpose

Vision is one of the tools that God uses to show us our purpose. He pulls back the curtain of eternity and gives us a glimpse of our purpose. The purpose of this is two-fold, it gives us a window seat into our own destiny from God's vantage point, because vision is essentially what God sees when He looks at us. And, secondly it confirms that our existence does indeed have meaning and value to someone greater than ourselves, which in turn is instant motivation and incentive to work towards the materializations of this future reality. When we see your life through God's eyes you see nothing but purpose, meaning, fulfillment and so much more. When our vision is properly aligned with God's vision there is nothing that seems impossible. When we see what God sees for us it is an innate motivator, it is almost as if our instincts are awakened by what we have just seen about our own lives. God masterfully uses this visual presentation of ourselves, to show us just enough to motivate us. He knows the right amount of vision to give us to satisfy our innate curiosity, but too much where it might have frightened us into complacency. Our Creator knows the right amount of vision to mete out to keep us properly balanced, because He knows the consequences of showing us too much too soon. Showing us too much too soon could be a severe shock to our system and we may become so overwhelmed by what we see that we don't believe it's even possible, or we begin to believe in so much that we make shipwreck trying to do ourselves what God can only do for us. In this pursuit of purpose, we have to trust the judgement of our Creator, because He has already declared that "He knows our beginning from our ending ... He knows our down sitting from our uprising." The question becomes do you trust God enough to allow Him to lead? Do you trust in God's ability to bring what He has shown you to past? The million-dollar question is, do you really trust God?

The problem with so many of us is that we're looking in all the wrong places to find the answers that only our Creator has the knowledge to give. Querying the wrong people about the meaning and purpose of your life will only lead you down the wrong path and what's unfortunate is that some people spend their entire lives looking in the wrong direction, walking down the wrong path that ultimately leads to nowhere. If only they would have taken the time to ask the Creator, they would've spent their time a bit more wisely and would've have been exponentially further ahead than where they are now, spinning their wheels but going absolutely nowhere.

I'm Here on Purpose

The existence of vision in the lives of humanity is two-fold, first and foremost it immediately confirms that our existence is not coincidental or accidental. Vision solidifies our existence by virtue of a pre-existing plan that was put in place before the foundation of the world. The purpose of vision is to confirm our existence; where sometimes we spend our lives looking for some type of validation, some type of confirmation that we are supposed to be here. And, we end up spinning our wheels looking for that thing that will bring us some type of peace or relief in knowing that our existence was intentional. But God uses vision to validate our existence and the second thing that vision does it reveals to us what are purpose is. Not only is our existence intentional but here's what I was put on this earth to do. What a travesty to spend your entire life in search of your purpose only to die never finding out what it is. Everyone wants to be able to say that they are here on purpose; everyone wants to be able to say that they belong here. And, vision gives every single person that God created the ability to do so. The reality is that you do belong here, you are here on purpose and don't let anyone tell you any different. God knew exactly what He was doing when He created you, and just because it is not clear what your purpose is right now doesn't mean that one day it won't become clear. You must continue getting closer to the Creator, because the closer you get to the Creator the closer you get to your purpose. The secret to discovering your purpose is directly tied to your proximity to the Creator, the further away from the Creator the more confused you will be about your identity. Likewise, the closer you are to the Creator the clearer your purpose will become. You can almost characterize this relationship with God as television reception and the antenna. The strength of the frequency is found in the proximity of the signal to the television. The stronger the signal the closer the frequency is to the television, which means the clearer the picture, audio etc. Much in the same way the signal is stronger the closer it is to the television, the closer we are to God the more we ultimately discover about ourselves. When you are not connected to the Creator there is no way you will ever figure out your purpose. Remember vision is what God sees when He looks at you, and Vision is what is revealed when you see yourself through God's eyes. So, how will you ever be able to see what God sees when you are not even connected to your Creator. The purpose of vision is to facilitate the revelation of purpose in the life of the visionary. Purpose is sometimes revealed through the ethereal window of the divine. The Creator pulls back the curtain of eternity and gives us a brief glimpse of our future. What an extraordinary experience to receive visual revelation of your purpose. God knows for some of us, "seeing is believing." And, so He shows us our future in order to incentivize our present. Essentially, God offers us visual motivation to keep moving in the direction that He has predestined for us to go. No one knows better than God what drives us, what motivates us, and what inspires us. He knows this, because He created us. And, no one knows us better than our Creator. Not only did He create us, but He also knows why He created us. Therefore, it makes all the sense in the world to get to know Him, because when you get to know Him, you essentially know all you need to know.

Purpose is the footing that all of us stand on when tackling the question of our existence. There is no other conceivable way to understand our existence than through the lens of purpose. Purpose is not just the undergirding of our existence, but it is the undergirding of the entire universe. The unity and harmony that is interwoven into creation unequivocally tells us that there was great thought and genus deposited into each and everything that exists in the universe. God is purpose personified, He is what purpose looks like when it needs an identity.

You Are Valuable

Your life is far too valuable to live it haphazardly, your life is far too important for you to end up a casualty. In the words Les Brown, "if you live life casually you will end up a casualty." No truer words have ever been spoken, because your life was a gift from God and there is no better way to show Him that you appreciate it than to do something with it. You owe it to yourself, you owe it to your Creator to grab all of the gusto that life has to offer. Not fulfilling your purpose, not fulfilling the visiony that God has set forth for your life is the same as wasting this precious life that God has given you. And what a tremendous gift to waste; a life that was freely given to you by the Creator; a purpose that He specifically had you in mind for you to fulfill; a vision that He only saw you being the executive of. Instead, you spent your entire life living out your own selfish self-interests, probably thinking to yourself "what right does God have to dictate to me what kind of life I'm supposed to lead?" How would He know more about what my life is than the actual owner of it? Two very interesting questions that this chapter was designed to answer. The Creator and the Giver of Life is uniquely poised to best answer the questions regarding our existence. He alone holds the most credibility when it comes to measuring out the vision and purpose for our lives. Not only does He have the answers but He is the answer when it comes to understanding the merits of our existence. Therefore, it behooves us to get to know Him, because the closer we get to Him the closer we get to seeing who we really are.

And, our lives were meant for so much more than fulfilling our own selfish self-interests. We were not created to serve ourselves, but we were created to serve others. This is why our purpose is intricately woven into the fabric of humanity, because our existence was designed to not make ourselves better but to make the world better. So, the consequences of us not doing what we were created to do is far greater and more reprehensible than just the lack of self-fulfillment, but the entire world suffers when we are not what we are supposed to be. The entire world is diminished when our purpose goes unfulfilled; the whole of mankind groans when we fall short of realizing God's vision for us. This why John Donne wrote,

> *"No man is an island entire of himself, every Msn is a part of the continent, a part of the main. So, if a man dies it diminishes*

me for I am involved with mankind. Therefore, never send to know for whom the bell tolls, it tolls for thee."

This is a universal call to action, because it expands our paradigm to think more of others than we do for ourselves. John is engaging us to think bigger than ourselves as it relates to the significance or the consequence of what we do, but redirect our attention towards the whole of mankind. This should drastically change the definition of purpose and vision from the intricacies and inner-workings of our own self-image to the magnanimous and universal outer-workings of all humanity. In essence, what I do or don't do doesn't just affect me, but it effects my brother, my sister; not just by blood or DNA, but throughout the whole of mankind. When we begin to globalize our purpose and our vision, we start to see that we were created to do more than just satisfy ourselves and make us happy. We were created for more than just to satisfy our own material pleasures, but we were created for the benefit of our fellow-man.

CHAPTER 2

THE DYNAMICS
OF VISION

"In the long run men hit only what they aim at. Therefore, though they should fail immediately, they had better aim at something higher …"

— Henry David Thoreau

I was recently watching my 2yr old daughter Lauren playing at the neighborhood playground and as I watched her I came across some helpful insights about vision that I thought I would share. Lauren saw a slide that she wanted to get on and so she begins tugging my hand in the direction of the slide and beckoning me by saying, "I wanna slide!" She moved me swiftly over to the slide from where we were. As we approached the slide I noticed her apprehension, as what may have appeared easy to do from a distance, became a bit harder the closer we got to it. I immediately begin encouraging her and telling her that she could do it and took her hand to help her on to the first step, but again I saw her apprehension rising. She wasn't moving as fast and I can hear a faint whining, which told me that I might have been moving faster than Lauren would've liked to go. What Lauren's was really doing was sizing up the slide in her little mind with relation to what she wanted to accomplish, which was slide down without any help from her daddy. But, she knew this was not going to happen right way, and I knew better than her that if she was going to gain the confidence to ride down the slide by herself she would need some help from her daddy.

Size Up

The first thing that stood out to me as I observed my daughter was that she began to "size up" the nature of this endeavor even before she took her first step. You must take the time to understand the gravity of the vision you are trying to pursue, because the size of the vision should be bigger than your belief in your ability to fulfill your vision by yourself. Your vision actually requires a partnership from God in order for it to be accomplished. And, this is why your vision always appears bigger than you can fathom believing in its achievability. Yes, it can be scary at first when you consider the magnificence and scope of this enterprise, but the size of your vision should cause you to automatically invite God to be a part of it. Your invitation to God is recognition that this cannot be accomplished without a power greater than you.

At 2yrs old she didn't try to conquer the slide in one fell swoop, but she slowly and gradually became acquainted with the territory before attempting to climb aboard. This is an important step in accomplishing any of your goals. You can't just expect to tackle a vision or a goal without first surveying the landscape of what you are endeavoring to accomplish and counting up the cost. You need to do some serious self-evaluation during this process, because accomplishing the goal might mean breaking it down into smaller more palatable steps that will make it more achievable. There must be some type of strategy or plan of action that comes out of the analysis of your vision. Everything begins and ends with a plan. You have to be able to strategically plan out the implementation of your vision. My daughter knew this even at 2yrs old, and the reason I know is because her initial approach to the slide was to get on the first step. Once on that first step she looked around and realized that she was no longer on the ground and I could hear her whining increase a bit. Lauren looked at the next step which was slightly higher than the first and she turned around and climbed back down to the ground. But she didn't stop there.

Never Stop

Oddly enough, this is another important step in accomplishing your visions, you cannot stop even when you have to take step a backwards to take another step forward. There will be times when you will get discouraged in the process and you may have to take a step backwards if nothing but to regroup and rethink through a strategy to get you to that next step. Never stop trying seems like pretty simple advice, but it is extremely critical when one is trying to achieve something. Never stop sizing up or resizing the nature of the goal you're trying to accomplish, because even though you may not get it in the first attempt, the victory comes in never giving up. She didn't stop and immediately lose interest because her goal of sliding down the slide unaccompanied was not accomplished immediately. Instead she got back up on the first step to try again at moving to the next one. After staring at the second step for a few minutes, I believe she built up enough nerve to try to take the next step, which she did. It's important to note at this juncture, the slide had three steps before you had to go through a small tunnel which takes you to top of the slide. Lauren stepped back down to the first step again and down to the ground a second time. You might've thought maybe this 2yr old has decided at this point that sliding down unaccompanied was not going to happen and it may be time to abort the mission. Not so! What she begins doing is cycling through climbing up the first two steps and climbing back down until she built up enough confidence to try the third step. Lauren used the concept of repetition to continue building up enough confidence to move to the next step. Yet another important point to consider when striving to achieve your goals. With each step, you are continuing to build up confidence in the process that will ultimately lead you to the finish line of your dreams. Success is a gradual process, and you must have patience to endure the process. Let's be even more frank, success is a process, nothing happens overnight. And when you are able to witness the pinnacle of someone else's achievements, it was not an overnight enterprise as the moment sometimes suggests. However, real success is coupled with a string of failures and setbacks that are just as much apart of the victories and achievements that success tends to bring. We tend to celebrate success at the end the process, because we clearly see the manifestation in front of us. But, the visionary can testify that before the actual culmination of their success, there was a series of sleepless nights, and restless moments; there was episodes of defeat they had to overcome. So never let anyone convince you that their success happened overnight or transpired on a whim; the only way you can truly believe that is if it was a very, very, very long night and they are using it as a metaphor to provide insight into the reality of their timeframe of success.

After Lauren got up enough confidence to try the next step, the next thing was the tunnel which she attempted to crawl through but didn't make it the first time. So, like other times before Lauren climbed back down to the ground to regroup. The process of vision was still taking place in Lauren's 2yr old mind, because whether I believed it or not she saw herself sliding down the slide without my help, and her determination and courage to keep trying convinced me of that; which brings me to my next point. The faith you have in your vision should be reflected in the determination and courage it takes to pursue it. People should be able to see the faith you have in your vision by how determined and courageous you are to achieve it. In doing so, you are bringing hope and inspiration to others to fulfill their dreams and visions as well. Our lives were designed to inspire others. If your life is not motivating and inspiring someone else's then you need to ask yourself, what am I here for? In fact, this question should be the catalyst to kickstart your vision. Why I am here, what was I put on this planet to accomplish, those should be two very important questions on the mind of every visionary, which they are willing to spend their entire life trying to answer. A groaning; a nagging desire to know what it is am I supposed to be doing, this should be the motivating piece for every potential visionary. This is where it starts, this is how it starts; and this dissatisfaction with not knowing the answer is now the driving force behind every decision that you make.

God Is Right There

You are probably wondering where was I throughout all of these attempts, I never left her side. And, I saw that it was time for me to intervene so that she wouldn't stop trying to achieve her goal. So, I offered her an incentive to keep trying by picking her up and placing her on the slide so she could experience going down the slide without all of the preliminary climbing. This serves as a foretaste of what was to come if you just keep on trying. God will sometimes give us a foretaste of what we are to become as we strive to endure the process as an incentive to continue. Herein lies the very definition of vision, when God peels back the curtain of time to show us a glimpse of who we are to become. He does this for several different reasons, one; to show us who He intended for us to be, two; to confirm that He actually does have a plan for our life and three; to incentivize this journey to our destination or our destiny. All three of these components are vital in us continuing in the direction that God has set forth for our lives to take. We will discuss this in even greater detail later in the book. But, God knows that He must coax us along sometimes because this journey can be a long arduous and meandering road at times. Sometimes, God will lift you up to the mountaintop for a few moments just so you can see that there really is a reward at the end. He doesn't give it all to us at once, but just enough to encourages us to continue in our pursuit of destiny.

After a few times of picking Lauren up and placing her on the slide to slide down again she was ready to give it a go for the steps again. By this time, the first two steps had almost become second nature because she had climbed them multiple times. And she was now on the third step staring at the tunnel starting to wince a bit before attempting to go through it. I started giving her some words of encouragement like, "C'mon Lauren" "You can do it" and in hearing that she looked back at me and smiled and begin to scurry through. When she looked at me I had climbed to the base of the third step so she could see that I was behind her- helping to build her confidence, as she attempted to go through the tunnel. Don't discount an encouraging word to help get you through the process. Sometimes it is from a friend, spouse, relative, coach or loved one and other times it is from a scripture, or a verse, a poem or quote from your favorite book or influential personality that helps to motivate you. We all need encouragement at one time or another, everyone needs to be inspired by something or someone. Often, it is from that inspiration that helps you to discover your realest potential. As I begin to encourage Lauren I could see her confidence continuing to build and now she had completely gone through the tunnel and she was at the top of the slide ready to take her first slide down.

Fear Is Essential

You probably thought that now that she was at the top of the slide she shouldn't have any more problems sliding down from there. Not so! I could see her apprehension rising up again, even after all she had accomplished. One would've thought that succeeding past the other steps would have convinced her that this was an achievable moment but quite to the contrary. Lauren was still afraid. It's important to note at this juncture that fear is going to accompany you throughout your entire journey through life. When you are striving to accomplish anything in life, fear will be an un-welcomed companion there to challenge you as well as steady your equilibrium in order to keep you balanced and humbled. Fear is not necessarily a bad thing all the time. Sometimes fear helps to keep us grounded. Fear serves as a harsh reminder of the reality of living, because success often times destabilizes us and causes us to think we are more than what we really are. The phenomenon of success can hurt some people more than it helps them. Sometime the more successes you have the more successful you become, the broader and riskier your thinking becomes the more your paradigm expands. The more invincible and arrogant you become-which are two destructive behaviors for a visionary, that ultimately leads to a very bad place. This is a Molotov cocktail of ego tripping that could be costly to you if fear does not accompany us on our journey.

Sensing Lauren's fear I moved from behind her on the third step to the side of the slide where she could see and hear her daddy encouraging her to continue. I told her to take my hand as she inched closer to the edge of the top of the slide. She took my hand and begin sliding down for the first time and when she made it to the bottom her smile was so big and bright that you could see the value of this step in the eyes of this two-year-old. We briefly celebrated her accomplishment, but she immediately returned to those three steps to try this slide again. Remember to celebrate the small achievements as you go through the process. It helps you to appreciate the steps that it took to get you to the finish line. I noticed this especially in small children, as you celebrate their small achievements it motivates them to do more; to try more. Children that are encouraged and positively motivated at a very young age tend to do better than those where the exact opposite has taken place.

Mission Accomplished

Before I knew it, Lauren was at the top of those stairs and through the small tunnel right back at the edge of the top of the slide she had just come down moments before. Yes, she was still a bit apprehensive at first but what was different this time is that she now has the memory of going down the slide before. Having that visual is yet another confidence builder she needed to slide down the slide a second time. This time she reached for my hand again to help her down the slide. Once down, we celebrated again and hurried back up those steps and through that tunnel a third time to do what she hadn't yet done in all of her attempts, to get down the slide without daddy's help. Each time she goes up the stairs and through the tunnel her confidence is being built. You have to learn to appreciate the lessons you receive in life. Every single day is a life lesson in a class where the entire world is it's pupils and the tougher the lesson the better the class. It's interesting what we retain and remember from our days in school. It's not those classes we skated through or skipped out of sheer boredom, but it is the classes and teachers that challenged us and forced us to stretch ourselves and our thinking. Those are the classes we tend to remember and such is life. It is those hard lessons, those tough lessons that helped to build our character and our integrity. The third time is a charm and Lauren finally went down the slide without any assistance from her father. And this time once she got to the bottom of the slide she started celebrating even before I could join in. Inasmuch as she realized better than anyone what it meant to finally go down this slide by herself. And she couldn't wait to try it again, this time faster with a bit more confidence than the last time with a little bit more skill this time than the last. You're probably thinking this story is nothing short of an embellishment from a proud father about his little girl sliding down a slide. While it is definitely a true story, it was my desire for you to appreciate the nuances of the steps towards Lauren's achievement of sliding down the slide by herself, and not the colorful way in which this feat was described. Who would've thought that so much could be learned from a such a simple activity and yet this is exactly what happened. The scriptures are true, "a little child shall lead them."

Dr. King & The Civil Rights Movement

I've often wondered how some people can work so diligently towards a goal; what is their motivation, what is the reward they are working for, and how are they able to summon the strength it takes to keep working at something where the reward seems to be nowhere in sight.?An observation I would imagine that is shared by many others, and many examples that we can use to examine and glean valuable tidbits and lessons that we can apply to our everyday lives. One such example is the Civil Rights Movement of the 1960's lead by the young, charismatic, intelligent and articulate leader Dr. Martin Luther King Jr. The Civil Rights Movement was birthed by and through the insistence and persistence of Black people to bring an end to racial discrimination and segregation in America. This was the long-term goal and reward that Black people were striving toward realizing with each march, each protest, and each demonstration. But, this reward would not be realized easily or conveniently, instead it would take much sacrifice, heartache, dedication, commitment, and even many causalities before this goal could ever be reached. This movement was comprised of many moments that served as inspiration and incentive to keep moving in pursuit of the ultimate goal of the eradication of racism and discrimination in the South. The bus boycott in Montgomery, AL was one such moment that help to galvanize and even propel the movement to heights unknown. It begins with the resistance of then seamstress Rosa Parks who refused to give her front seat on a crowded bus to a white man and move to the back. Her refusal to give up her seat sparked a firestorm of attention from both the black and white community. At the time a young, black minister by the name of Rev. Dr. Martin Luther King Jr. was made aware of this altercation on a crowded Montgomery Bus, who called a meeting with local leaders to devise a plan of action. It was determined that a mass boycott of all city buses was to begin with all blacks in Montgomery taking alternate transportation to targett the economy of this segregated municipality. Car pools and other black supported alternate modes of transportation was used to send a message to the white politicians and citizens of Montgomery that blacks were not going to take this fight lying down. This boycott took enormous patience for the final victory was ever realized. What started as an experimental respite eventually became a year-long campaign to desegregate the bus system in Montgomery. The final result; after months of struggling, marching and fighting to desegregate the bus system in Montgomery, victory was finally realized through the Supreme Court of the United States, that discrimination on local city buses was unconstitutional and had to immediately cease.

Many books have been written and TV shows and movies produced to highlight the accomplishments of the Civil Rights Movement. And, the tenets and principles of the movement have been discussed ad-nauseam, however, I want to discuss the movement in more general terms. We want to look at the movement and its various moments as an extraordinary measurement of strength and determination to ultimately get to the goal of the removal of Jim Crow laws and statutes in the South. The kind of endurance, tenacity and determination that it took to continue marching, boycotting and fighting for equality, justice and fairness had to be just as extraordinary as the rewards they sought. This movement took patience, it took sacrifice, it took faith, it took determination, it took courage, and what's interesting is these are the same things that are needed for us to realize the goals that we've set for ourselves. When you look at the tremendous faith that Dr. King had to continue to motivate the same black people that he needed to help push the movement forward. Countless speeches and sermons he wrote and preached to articulate the plight of the Negro in the South. Dr. King knew that black people needed a spokesperson, someone that would vocalize their struggles and their sentiments to White America. A leader who could not only articulate a plan of action but implement it as well. He became the leader that black people needed to get them to the Promise Land that Dr. King proclaimed he saw in his last speech he gave in a Memphis, Tennessee Church that stormy April night the eve of his assassination. He declared,

"I don't know what will happen now, we've got some difficult days ahead. But, it really doesn't matter with me now because I've been to the Mountaintop. And, I don't mind ... like anybody I would like to live a long-life longevity has its place. But, I'm not concerned about that now I just want to do God's will. And, He's allowed me to go up into that mountain and I've looked over and seen the Promise Land. I may not get there with

*you, but I want you to know tonight that we as people will get to
the Promise Land. So, I'm happy tonight I'm not worried about
anything, I'm not fearing any man, mine eyes have seen the glory
of the coming of the Lord."*

The Promise Land that Dr. King spoke of could have been
purely metaphorical or it could have actually been a vision
that he experienced where he witnessed the culmination of
all his hard work and determination towards a movement
that has impacted so many people. I tend to believe that
this Promise Land was not purely metaphorical or symbolic
or that was only inserted into this sermon for aesthetic
purposes, but it was an actual vision that Dr. King had
where God showed him some intimate and private things
about not only his own life, but the lives of those who died in
the movement before him. And, this vision was an inspiring
and motivational moment for the hundreds of black people
that were packed into that small church to hear what later
became Dr. King's last sermon of record entitled, "I've Been
to The Mountain Top." In fact, it was a message that he
almost never gave, because as the story goes, Dr. King was
scheduled to speak the evening of April 3rd but because of
the tremendous storms that night, he didn't think the service
would be well attended. So, he instructed his "longtime
friend and associate" Ralph Abernathy to go and speak
in his stead. However, when Ralph arrived at the church
he was to speak at, he was overwhelmed by the enormous
crowd that had gathered despite the storm warning. And,
he immediately got on the phone and called Dr. King and
told him of his observations and that the people gathered
was not a crowd for him but these people came out to hear
Dr. King. After speaking to Dr. King, Ralph convinced
this movement's leader to come and to rally the troops in

what would ultimately be his last time. The impact of this speech that stormy evening reverberated throughout the entire movement. It was that fateful day on April 4th that Dr. King's speech became a prophecy of things to come, because it was at the Lorraine Motel in Memphis, Tenn. where he met an assassin's bullet that ended his life, and caused some to wonder if he knew that his time was about to be up. The Promise Land that Dr. King spoke of the night before became a reminder to some after they heard of his untimely death that his speech may have been a precursor of what was to come. That Dr. King was in some way letting us in on a moment that he was already aware of and prepared for, a moment that God-Himself may have revealed to him earlier.

The Now Generation Meets Vision

We live in what many might call the "Now Generation" time and technology have intersected to produce a moment where what we desire is literally at our fingertips. Gone are days of waiting for something to arrive or to materialize; gone are the days of patiently waiting for something to happen, we are experiencing a unique moment in time where what we desire is right within our reach. When you think about how far technology has progressed and as a result how far technology has taken us as a humanity, technology has brought us to a place where we have never been before. The word "instant" has taken on a new meaning for many of us, what we want we can get in an instant. Social media has made information even more accessible, you can find people and get information almost instantaneously. We have fast food, microwave ovens, smart phones, smart TVs and the list goes on and on. So, it seems that the "Now Generation" has intersected with vision, because what technology has produced is a fast food appetite that vision cannot and will not immediately gratify. There is a patience that is required with vision that in some cases keeps the visionary hungry and determined until the vision eventually comes to pass. Vision explicitly and implicitly demands patience; vision requires a plan of action or a strategy that needs time in order to materialize. Vision means that what I'm working towards is worth waiting for; it means that I possess the patience to not only see what I want to happen but to work towards making it a reality. Vision also denotes some level of stability as well, inasmuch as it takes discipline to map out a plan of action and to see it through from concept to reality.

For those of the "Now Generation" they are more concerned with what's happening in the moment rather than planning for tomorrow. For them the present is far more tantalizing than the future, and yes, it is easy to see how this can happen. We are a very visual people and sometimes looking at our today is far more palatable than seeing a tomorrow that s appears to be many moons away. Seeing what other people can't see might mean working harder than others are willing to work. Vision is what keeps you up at night, it's your motivation to keep going when everything and everyone around you is telling you to quit. Vision means I'm working towards a goal that I can only see right now, but one that everyone will see one day.

Immediate gratification is one of the by-products or the consequences of the technological advances of the times we are currently experiences. Our wants and desires can in many cases be satisfied in a short approximation of time, because of some of the advances that technology has produced. For example, "Google" has become the world's foremost search engine when it comes to finding out information about any and everything, when it used to be your local library where you can go to find information about any and everything. But, the instantaneous prospect of getting the information you want without having to go outside of your house or drive to another location to find what you're looking for is far more gratifying and titillating. As quickly as you have typed in the questions or in some cases; depending on the type of devices you're using, audibly queried "Google" the answer is sent back in minutes, sometimes even seconds. The impact of this type of exchange with the World Wide Web has had some interesting repercussions; we've taken information completely for granted, and the reliability on technology has become even greater in the twenty-first century.

So, we are constantly being challenged by what we see now vs. what we expect to experience in the future. There is a constant choice that we're confronted with in our lives about the present and the future. And, many of us are so overwhelmed by our now that we can't even think about what might happen tomorrow or later on down the road. We see this happening quite often amongst our young people, because there at an interesting moment in history, where time is no longer an obstacle to our wants and desires. There was a point in time where you had to wait to receive certain things, you had to wait for your birthday or Christmas to come around before you could get this or that. You had to wait on invention or innovation to catch up with the times before some of what you dreamed was even possible. But, now that we are here and waiting is no longer necessary, because innovation and invention are in-sync with the machinations of the day, our hearts desires are only dwarfed by money, demand or both. What impact has that had on making plans for the future? How has what is happening now effected plans for tomorrow? That is a question that only this generation can answer, but as an ardent observer, it seems like the mantra is enjoy now, pay later. Why worry about the future when you can enjoy yourself today?

In this context, of having a vision seems like a more adult term, and adult not necessarily in age but in mindset. It takes an adult mindset to have vision; a vision that extends beyond your present set of circumstances; a vision that even extends beyond your own mortality. When someone has a vision beyond their physical existence that is somebody who is thinking not just about themselves, but those who will be coming after them. Legacy planning is one of way of looking at this type of behavior, which is what you find from people who have a considerable amount of wealth, or they have some fame or achieved some notoriety and they are now thinking about the posterity of their name. What will they say about me when I'm gone? Who will I leave my inheritance to when I'm gone, who will I pass the mantle of leadership to when I'm gone? These are all questions that are usually considered by those who are dutifully engaged in thinking about life after they're gone. These are not necessarily morbid considerations, but they are necessary considerations nonetheless.

Vision Takes Faith

When you look at the life of Abraham; 'The Father of Faith," the Bible describes as one who had an immense faith in God, and how God used him mightily in his day and in his time. God would talk with Abraham in dreams and visions. And, God would share with Abraham His plans for his life. God spoke candidly with Abraham about how He would make his name great, and by the sands of the seashore those would be the accumulated prospect of his seed. What's interesting about these talks with God about Abraham's future was that he was not a young man. Abraham was well into his twilight years when God begin speaking to him about his future. One would think that a man in his 70 or 80s would be done with work and once finished would then think about his posterity or his legacy. But, at 75yrs of age, Abraham didn't have a legacy, Abraham didn't have any children to leave any of his inheritance to and Sarah; his wife, was barren. And, God was speaking to Abraham about a seed that would exceed the numbers of the stars in the sky or the sands on the seashore, but Abraham was well into his twilight years and his wife was barren. The bible says that Abraham never questioned God, but absorbed all that was spoken into his life. However, my imagination always gets the best of me when thinking about the thoughts that were probably running through the mind of Abraham as God was revealing to him the plans about his life. Abraham was probably thinking to himself, why is God talking to me about a lineage or a heritage and I'm in my old age? How is God planning to bless me with seed and my wife cannot even have children? When you review the life of Abraham and the dynamic of God talking to him about the size of his seed and tremendous legacy and heritage you will leave behind, one cannot help but wonder how Abraham maintained his faith when there was no real evidence of this ever happening. Through the luxury of time we see that Abraham never lived to see the fulfillment of God's promise, but the Word of God said, that he never wavered in his faith in God's ability to bring it to pass. God was essentially telling Abraham about a space in time that he would no longer be alive, but his name would still resonate with the lives of those he touched. It is a natural proclivity for us to be excited about the prospect of something happening, especially when the assumption is we will be able to physically experience it. But, it is a different thing entirely when you are told of something that is going to take place, but you will not be alive to appreciate it. God, however, never provided Abraham with a timeline or a timeframe in which this would take place, nor did He reveal Abraham's life expectancy as it relates to the fulfillment of this promise. But, Abraham was still expected to have the same faith in God as if he would be there to see the realization of what God had promised. This is probably why God didn't divulge to much information about Abraham's life expectancy or the timeframe of His promise, to not interfere with Abraham's faith in His word. Inasmuch, it would be hard to believe that Abraham; if he knew he wouldn't be alive to see the posterity of his seed, that he would not have wavered in his faith in God. So, yes there is a human element to having faith. You have to be able to juxtapose between your reality and the future God's has promised, and decide if you're going to believe in your reality or I am going to believe in the promise of God. Your reality is actually the tangible component that your faith is constantly confronted with even as you are reminded of what God promised you for the future. This is why, faith is as "real" as anything you can feel or touch, because the transformation that takes place in your life is evidence of the power that faith contains.

Of course, Abraham didn't know at the time that in the mind of God, he would not be alive to witness the fruits of his innumerable seed that would bear his name. All he had was the faith in God to believe that He was able to bring to pass everything that He said He would. But, never did God say that Abraham would be alive to see it materialize. Abraham, would have to be here for it to begin or else it wouldn't be His seed. So, that part of it might have been a given, but the part that Abraham had to completely trust God for was to fulfill his promise of an innumerable seed, even if he may not be alive to see accomplished. God was true to his promise, and gave Abraham a son that he called "Isaac," which ultimately became the seed that would produce even more seed. This is where "vision" intersects with "faith" because you need both in order to believe in a God who is shown you something that you can't naturally see, but you believe in your spirit it's going to come to pass. The vision is God granting you a peak behind the curtain of time and eternity to see what He's already done. And, the faith comes in when you see the finished product in the spirit before you ever see in the flesh.

Abraham Meets His 20th Century Contemporary

Much like the story of Abraham, Dr. King didn't see the final rewards of his struggle and sacrifice, but died believing in the inevitable realization of those rewards because of the tremendous faith that he had in God. And, I believe Dr. King's faith was validated before his death as he eluded to his vision of the Mountaintop, which I believe included those people of the movement that had gone before and those of the movement Dr. King would ultimately leave behind. Dr. King's faith in God afforded him the confidence in knowing that as he put it "unearned suffering is redemptive." And, that one-day black people would reap the rewards of their immense sacrifice of the movement. These rewards appeared "opened-ended" although implicit within most of his sermons and speeches were themes like equality, justice and unity. The specifics of these broad themes are still being meted out in the lives of everyday black people, and in many cases, still remain to be seen. However, the movement itself was focused on voting rights, civil rights, fair housing, and the elimination of segregation and discrimination in all its forms throughout the South and even parts of the North.

Abraham, much like Dr. King didn't live to see the offspring of his faith as God had promised Abraham he would be the father of. His name itself was changed from Abram to Abraham, because he would be the "Father of Many Nations." God told Abraham that his offspring would rival the sands of the seashore which are innumerable. Although, what is interesting about God's promises to Abraham was they were made to him when he was well into his 70's & 80's and past his child rearing years. In fact, his wife Sarah was in her twilight years as well. So, for God to make these promises to essentially two very old people that they would be the father and mother of many nations seems extremely implausible given their age and life expectancy. But, that was indeed the miracle behind God's promise, because it was not predicated on Abraham or Sarah's age or physical condition, but it was thoroughly contingent upon the divine power of the God their faith rested in.

Vision Takes Patience

Essentially the plan that God has for us is going to take patience and sacrifice, two of the hardest and most intolerable words for a cCild of God to come to grips with. You need both if you are going to have an effective and impactful relationship with God. When you think about the sacrifice and struggle that accompanies any reward or blessing from God, the enormity of the sacrifice is usually an indication of the size of the blessing. But, it is the waiting period in the midst of the trial, or in the midst of the test that measures your ability to survive and receive what God has in store for you. From a practical standpoint, the depth of sacrifice whether it be natural, mental or spiritual usually determines the size of the reward. And, this principle works across all facets of life. When a person endeavors to go on a diet to lose weight and they decide to stop eating a certain kind of food; coupled with the diet is an accompanying regiment of exercise, if the diet and exercise is adhered to then the reward is tremendous. The secret is in the follow-through, in order to obtain or accomplish any type of goal or objective the key is in the follow-through. If you are able to endure the sacrifice that encompasses your dream or vision, you will see the realization of it because of your ability to follow-through. Professional athletes that are successful at their craft do so because of their ability to follow-through. Their ability to endure the rigorous training and practices to hone their athletic skill and innate ability is the key to their ultimate success in the end. The marvelous part in all this is that the viewing public is treated to this athlete's tremendous skill after countless hours of training and practice, and we assume that the athlete's innate ability is the overriding reason for their success. However, what we discover is that their success on the field is a direct result of what they did off the field; a combination of their innate ability and their commitment to training and developing themselves to compete at the highest level. We don't see the practices, we don't see the training, we are not there for the workout sessions, we are not up for the early morning runs. But, it is all of these things and more that result in the overwhelming success that appears to be driven by their innate God-given ability, but it is actually their commitment to sacrifice that yields these great rewards. Essentially willing to lose in order to gain is the fundamental principle in all of this, you have to be willing to give up something in order to get something. So, the question really becomes what are you willing to give up, what are you willing to sacrifice? You have to be willing to commit to the sweat equity that will ultimately result in reaching what was once an unattainable goal. But, because of my willingness to sacrifice as great as the reward that I desire to receive what was once unattainable is now within my reach, what was once insurmountable is not within striking distance. And this principle can be applied to every facet of life; it is not limited to just the sports arena, but entertainment, business, entrepreneurship, politics, and so much more.

Chapter 3

GOD'S VISION

For I know the thoughts that I think toward you, saith the Lord,
thoughts of peace, and not of evil, to give you an expected end."
- Jeremiah 29:11 KJV

In Bruce Almighty, we see the hilariously funny Jim Carey play an arrogant, self-absorbed news anchor consumed with becoming the next news anchor that he will stop at nothing to turn his dream into a reality. Even coming into a chance encounter with God-Himself, played by Morgan Freeman. Bruce Nolan is Jim's character that happens upon a maintenance man in an abandon building that turns out to be the proverbial "Man Upstairs." Bruce was summoned by God for this meeting after having been so consumed with his own life's ambitions that he wanted a meet and greet with "The Man" Himself. After complaining and criticizing the work that God had been doing in His life, Bruce concluded that if He were God he could do a better job. Much to Bruce's surprise God was up for the challenge, and according to God, was looking forward to the vacation. Bruce highly underestimated the responsibility of being God; like most of us do, and he only looked at God's role through the lens of his own limited perspective. So, what God decided to do as a lesson to Bruce was to give Bruce a taste of what it actually feels like to be God. At first, Bruce jumped at the chance to be endowed with the powers of the Supreme Being; able to do what you wanted, when he wanted and not have to ask anybody for permission to make it happen. Bruce; like many of us, first begin by righting some of the proverbial wrongs in his own life. Meddling and interfering in his own work environment to move his self into the anchor seat at the news station, and manipulating his relationship with his then girlfriend Grace; played by Jennifer Aniston, to win her undying devotion to-you guessed it, him.

Me, Myself &. Bruce

With all of these newly endowed powers, Bruce did like many of us would, "take thee care of number 1." After all, we are the ones that matter the most from our perspective. There is no one more important in our eyes than ourselves. And, having the powers of the "Almighty" only motivates us even more to take care of those things that we feel should've been done by God already. We are not interested in the reasoning or explanation that God has for not giving us what we want when we want it, our only concern is getting what we want now that we have the power to do it for ourselves. Being endowed with God's powers, His Omniscience (All Knowing), Omnipresent (Everywhere at all times) and Omnipotent (All Powerful), gives Bruce the superiority that he believes he deserves. Again, this is all from a very selfish perspective, only seeing life through your eyes is a very limited and narrow-minded view of not just you but the world around you. Bruce used this unique opportunity to get revenge and pounce on people he wouldn't be able to under normal circumstances, if it were not for his divine powers. He soon learned that God's powers are not meant to be used so selfishly, but they are meant to be used for the greater good. A reality, Bruce very quickly was introduced to as he was just getting used to being the one with all of the power. And, Bruce is like many of us who dream and wish; if just for one day, we were given the powers of the "Almighty," and we could do whatever we want to whoever we want without any consequence or concern for retribution. Everyone who ever stood in our way of being great or being what we wanted to be were the first ones on our list for revenge. Our wishes and our desires would take preeminence over any and everyone else's. There would be no need greater than ours, and everyone else would have to wait in line before their needs or concerns were met or addressed. In fact, in our limited view of what God's job is, there is no one else that mattered but "US." Being God; in our eyes, was having God's powers to do with them whatever we want only for the betterment of ourselves. The 1st law of nature is "survival of the fittest," so it seems quite befitting for us; if given these divine powers, to take care of ourselves. It is a natural instinct for us to consider ourselves over others and this is why it doesn't seem that far-fetched for us to be preoccupied with fulfilling our own agenda over the wants and desires of someone else.

According to our Hollywood example, in "Bruce Almighty" it is only when Bruce is forced to handle the tens of millions of problems that others are dealing with that he starts to understand the gravity of the position he now holds. He begins hearing faint murmurings in his ear at inopportune times and could not figure out what they were or where they were coming from. And, it wasn't until he had a pow-wow with the "Main Upstairs" that he discovered these were the prayers of the millions of believers that Bruce was neglecting by being so preoccupied with his own selfish pursuits. It wasn't until he begins to see the indirect consequences of his actions and how they impacted the lives of others that he starts to realize the magnitude of the power he now holds. In a sense, it wasn't until Bruce was confronted with the problems of other people that he had to handle that he begins to realize the tremendous weight of the position that God-Himself holds with mankind. It is not a position or role to be taken lightly and not one that should be engaged selfishly.

So Many Questions

Why does life have to be so complicated? Why does life have to be so complex? For every question, there seems to be even more questions that can be asked before an adequate answer is given. It seems from our perspective, life is as Dr. King so eloquently asserted in his famous "A Knock at Midnight" sermon,

> "...a tale told by an idiot full of sound in fury signifying nothing, so many people find themselves crying out with the philosopher Schopenhauer that life is an endless pain with a painful end. So many people find themselves crying out with Paul Lawrence Dunbar's Crust O' bread and a corner to sleep in, a minute to smile and an hour to weep in, a pint of joy to a

peck of sorrow and never to laugh but the moans come double and that is life."

This is a poet's expression of the pain and sorrow that life seems to bring to all of us. A pain and agony that is as necessary as the strength and power it eventually brings. But, why does life have to be this way? Why do we have to experience the tumultuous ups and downs of life, why can't life just be one steady and straight path to our destination? One writer surmised about this very quandary and concluded, "*if* you know the "why" of living, you can endure anyhow." And, this does make perfect sense, for the most of us, if we knew the meaning behind our struggles, if we knew why we had disappointments, if we knew why we had setbacks, if we knew why we had to experience pain, it would probably be a little easier to endure. In a general sense, we do know why we are going to have to experience pain, and it is primarily because in life we are going to have some good days and bad days. Generally speaking, everyone knows this reality of life, but even in knowing this we still seem to have a myriad of questions. But with regards to the writer's own words in a literal sense if we knew "why" we have disappointments, and why we have pain it might give us more of an incentive to press on. Emphasis on the word "might" because the "why" might not always be a happy ending and knowing "why" may not always provide the necessary incentive to endure as we initially hoped. And, sometimes we only find out after we have experienced the pain of a loss, or experienced the heartache of a failure, that we discover what was really going on. If we knew the moment, the very instant we had to go through; why this experience was necessary, then it would probably make the pain a little more bearable, or so we think. Knowing the "why" the very minute, the very second, we had to experience pain would probably make the experience more palatable. The "why" for us is the incentive that we need to consent to going through the process; we need to know "why?" Similar to the way a spoiled child who instead of just following their parent's specific instructions continuously ask the question "why?" The reality is that God doesn't need our "buy-in" in order to take us through an experience that He deems is necessary for us to go from one level to the next. Our only job in this relationship with Him is to just trust that He knows what He's doing, and He's able to get us from point A to B. Knowing the why; for us, in some ways insulates us during the process, because we now have some information about the process that might help us to get through it.

But, does knowing in advance of somethings make it better for us to deal with? Does knowing in advance of a loved one's death make it less painful a loss? Does knowing in advance of a disappointment or a major setback, make the impact easier to comprehend? There must be something to God not always letting us in on the purpose behind our struggles that is all a part of His divine plan as well. The experience is just part of it, but the purpose is really at the heart of what everyone seems to want to know. And, yes this is no secret to God. He knows that we want to know "why?" He knows about our incessant whining and criticisms of the process. He knows how badly you want to know why you were born in this family and not the other one. He knows how badly you want to know why you weren't born with a silver spoon in your mouth. He knows how much you want to know why you were born with a mental disorder or physical deformity, not knowing makes life even harder. Yes, God knows! God knowing the answers to these questions, and Him not revealing them to us, doesn't make Him a bad God. It makes Him a purposeful God. Withholding this information from us doesn't mean that God doesn't love or care about us, but it means that His plan for our life is more complex and complicated than we think. Sometimes God does tell us why some things happened to us, or we find out on the other side of victory why the experience of defeat was necessary. But, essentially it is all a part of the process or the plan that God has for each and every one of our lives.

God Doesn't Need Our Consent

God not needing our "buy in"is the same as God not needing our permission to do to us what He deems necessary to get us to where He wants us to be. As the Creator of heaven and earth and everything in between, God does not need to ask our permission to afflict us. The one thing that we do know about God is that everything He does is for a purpose, so if He does afflict us it is for a greater and much larger purpose than we have yet to realize. So, we can't get so caught up in the process that we lose sight of our ability to trust God who is the Author and Finisher of the process as well as our faith. Not asking our permission is directly a result of Him wanting our trust in Him to be greater than the desire for us to resist being afflicted. Essentially, God is asking us through the vicissitudes and perils of life, "Do you trust me?" Trusting is what is most important to God, because He wants to know that you trust His plans for your life even if you don't agree with. He knows that He is the best person for us. He knows that no one has better plans for you than He does. But, what is most important to Him is that you believe that about Him first even before it is proven through the crucible of experience. That is the very definition and expression of our faith in Him to be able to trust His plans, His direction, His will for our lives over our own even before He proves His trustworthiness through the inevitability of experience. Experience is an inevitability of life, which cause Job to declare in the 14th Chapter and verse 1 of the book that bears his name in the Holy Writ, "man that is born of a woman is of a few days and full of trouble." And, who better to tell us about faith and affliction than Job, after all he is considered the poster child for suffering. But, Job had faith in God, before, after and most importantly during the timeframe he was being afflicted. Job continued to believe in God's plans for His life. Never wavered in his faith in God, but continued to believe that his suffering was purposeful and once God was through with him, he would come out as pure gold. Job held on to this belief even despite his three friends; Eliphaz the Temanite, Bildad the Shuhite and Zophar the Naamathite, who supposedly came by to console him, but really came by to ridicule him and pass judgement on him.

You have to be careful of those who claim to be your friends, because sometimes they are only carriers of the title but occupy hidden agendas and motives. Everybody is not going to be happy for you. Everybody is not happy to see you succeed; everybody is not happy to see you cross the finish line; everybody will not celebrate with. And, Job's case, everybody will not comfort you; everybody will not give you an encouraging word; everybody will not be there to uplift you, even your so-called friends. So, in this process of fulfillment we can't get caught up in what things look like on the surface, but every day we've got to resolve to look a little deeper.

My Plans Are Better Than Your Plans

In the opening verses of Psalms 23, verse 1 (KJV) David says "The Lord is my Shepherd and I shall not want. He maketh me to lie down in green pastures." Every child who's matriculated through Sunday School should know this chapter, or at the very the least this first verse. And, yet it is one of the most quoted and the least understood verses in the Bible. The second clause of this verse is where all of my attention is drawn, "He maketh me to lie down in green pastures." Why does God have to make you lie down in green pastures? If the pastures are green then they would denote they are worthy of my company and I would want to lie down in them. When I first begin to really think about this scripture and examine it's real meaning, the Lord showed me that His green pastures are different that our green pastures and therein lies the pushback or the hesitation to inhabit or to rest in areas that God has desired verses places that we have picked out ourselves. It is a natural inclination or propensity for us to think we know what's best for ourselves over any one else in our lives. No one can tell us better than we can what is best for us. And, this is essentially what David is saying in verse 1 of Psalms 23, that if God is considered to be my Shepherd and I shall not want, then the expectation is that He should know more about my life than I do and that He would know what's best for me even better than I would. Consequently, If He is my Shepherd in the first clause of verse 1 and I'm still telling Him where is the best place for me to lay down, then is He really my Shepherd? Implicit within this scripture is God's ability to see further down the road of our life then we can, even though this is a reality that most people are not willing to admit. Subsequently, if God can see further than I can, then He should be the one I'm trusting to be my Shepherd over anybody else. This verse also expresses the constant tension that exist between our will and God's will for us. David in this Psalm has characterized us as sheep, and the sheep do not typically know as much or more than the Shepherd. The reason why we have a Shepherd is because we lack the intellect or the wherewithal to determine where to go, and therefore we need him to lead us; sometimes, in areas or places that we don't want to go. The sheep depend on the Shepherd for their very survival. And, sometimes the pastures that the Shepherd leads us into are not what we would we have chosen for ourselves. We think we know a better place to lay down and rest, but the reality is the places we have chosen only looked green from a distance but the closer you get to them you see they were full of weeds. The reality is we don't know what is truly best for us and that is why we need God to lead us. His sight is better than our sight. His vision is better than our vision. He can see further than we can. He can see much more than we can. And, what's interesting is that even though we may know all of this about the Shepherd's vision verses our own, we are still more willing to trust our own sight over the Shepherd's. We are still more willing to trust our vision over the Shepherd's, we are still more willing to trust our will over the Shepherd's. Not only did He say He knows the way, but He is the way. The fact of the matter is, we really don't know that we don't know and that is a dangerous place to be in. Not only do we not know, but we are far too stubborn to admit we don't know. It's one thing to not know something and be honest enough to admit not knowing. But, it's another thing entirely to not know something and be too stubborn to admit not knowing. And, often because of our stubbornness God has to make us do what we what we wouldn't normally do because of the nature of our relationship with Him. He makes us lie down in places that are green even before we're able to see they are green ourselves. What an interesting relationship that we-as sheep, have with the Shepherd. One would think there would be more of an innate reliance on the knowledge and leadership of the Shepherd, however the exact opposite is true, the sheep are claiming to know just as much or more than the Shepherd.

Not only is God's will and our will diametrically opposed to one another, in that it almost appears we want different things for the same person but our spiritual reality is polar opposites as well. The truth of the matter is we cannot handle the truth of where we really are spiritually, and the only one that really knows the truth is God. And, this is the reason why God has to spoon-feed us our destiny, because if He gave it to us in one big healthy portion, the reality is we couldn't handle it. In fact, the larger reality is, what we can handle and we what we think we can handle are completely different as well. The last person that we are honest with, which also happens to be the first-person Shakespeare said we should be true to, is ourselves. His exact words were, "to thine own selves be true." We owe it to ourselves to be true to ourselves. But, most times we are not. The first person that we lie to is ourselves and no one know this better than God does.

Can You Trust Him?

The reason God doesn't give us everything at once is because we simply can't handle it. Regardless of what we say we can handle or not, God knows the truth and not only does He know the truth but He also knows our ending from our beginning. And, if He's the one that knows our ending from our beginning and He's decided that He's going to facilitate the dissemination of that information to us, then all we can do is trust that He knows what He's doing. I know that it is easier said than done especially when we are left to experience the impact of a loss or a tragedy or a setback often times without an explanation or even a warning that it is coming, and God continues to ask in the midst of the process "do you trust me?" That's a hard question to answer when you don't have anything else to go on but your faith in God, that you can't see but is constantly asked to believe in. It seems unfair to ask us to believe in someone that offers very little information about your purpose. On the surface, that would appear to be a pretty one-sided type of relationship, with one person asking so much of you and controls how much information you know about them. In our terrestrial relationships, we tend to have problems with people that ask so much of everyone else but seem to be unwilling to do anything themselves. They want you to believe in them and to take their word that they are who they say they are and they are not going to let you down. People want you to put your faith in them, when they make promises and you take their word only to be let down time and time again. The bold reality is that a person's word is only as good as their willingness to follow-through on what they said. And, even that is no guarantee, because any number of things could have happened to alter their words, or cause them to change what they've said given the new set of circumstances.

God, on the other hand not only wants us to trust in Him because of what He knows, but also trust Him because of

His ability. You see it's important to note at this juncture that God knowing our beginning from our ending is not coincidental. He didn't just happen to be in the right place at the right time for this information to be disclosed or given, but He is the Author of the beginning and the ending. So, when He asks us to trust Him, He's not asking us to trust Him just because of what He knows, but He's also asking us to trust in His ability to bring what He knows to pass. This is what separates God from man, because man can make all kinds of promises and sell all kinds of "wolf tickets" and say this and that, but man's ability to follow-through is limited because of the finite and fallible minds and capacities to accomplish what we said we wanted to accomplish. Regardless of what you believe or have been told, we are not ultimately in control of everything, so our words are not as powerful as someone who does have control over any and everything. Our abilities are limited, our capabilities, our mind is limited, our body is limited thereby making what we say limited as well. Subsequently, we shouldn't be surprised when man disappoints us, we shouldn't be taken by surprised when man lets us down, we shouldn't become weary when man fails us, because it is in our human nature to do so. We are fallible, finite beings that need God to lead us and to guide us into all truth. However, when God ask you to trust Him, He's not asking you to just trust Him based on what He knows, or what He's already done, but to trust His follow-through. God is the epitome of a "Promise Keeper." He never breaks a promise. He never makes a mistake or does anything that is wrong. He is beyond reproach. This is why God can demand so much from us, because He is capable of doing so much. The song writer rightfully declared, "He's Got the Whole World in His Hands." The prophet Isaiah declared in the book that bears his name chapter 46 and verse 10, (KJV) "Declaring the end from the beginning and from ancient time those things that are not yet done saying, my counsel shall stand I will do all my pleasure." So, you are not believing in a God who is limited in abilities, you are not asked to believe in a God whose existence or power is dependent upon an indeterminate number of factors, you are not asked to believe in a God that is bound by time and circumstance. Our God stands outside of time and dictates to time what will and what will not take place.

It is very important for us to understand God's role in all of this, He is not an inconsequential figure that happened to be in the right place and the right time to obtain all of this important information about the lives of everyone that ever lived and because He has all of this information we should trust Him. Not So! God is not merely a tour guide in our lives only providing us with insights He-Himself was given by another source, but He is the SOURCE and not just the source but the Author or the Creator of the information about our lives that we seek. Therefore, God's credibility is un-matched; His role as the Creator of everything trumps any other competing force that claims to have as much or even more information than God does; whoever that might be. Essentially, when you know God you know everyone and everything you need to know. Subsequently, it behooves you to get to know Him, because in Him resides our purpose, our destiny, our peace, the answer to life's questions and more importantly the person He created us to be.

What Is Vision?

Vision; from a spiritual perspective, is God's eyesight for our lives, it is essentially what God sees when He is looking at the person He wants us to be. God's Vision is not like ours, because He has the ability to not only see the future, but He can also impact the end results of the future. When God endows us with a vision, He is actually giving us a glimpse of the person we are to become. He is literally pulling back the curtains of time and letting us in on a secret that only He knows. In fact, the reason that God can love us in the midst of our mess is because when He looks at us He doesn't see the person we are He sees the person that we are to become. Our future lives are a constant reminder to God of the potential He created when He decided to include us in His plan for creation. Our lives were meant for something; our lives were meant to matter, not just White ones, but Black one's too; not just Hispanic ones by Asian one's too. In God's eyes, all lives were meant to matter, all lives were created for a reason and for a purpose. they were meant for something bigger, something better, and something greater.

And, vision is God's way of giving us a glimpse of who we really are. It is extremely important that we all were given vision, because identity and vision are closely related. In order to fulfill your vision, you have got to know who you are. You can't even fathom the real meaning of vision, until you fully understand who you are in God. The importance of vision also solidifies the impact of the consequences of Adam and Eve's disobedience in the Garden of Eden. One of the greatest things that we loss on the dreadful day in the Garden was our own identity. We loss the very thing that made us great in God's eyes, the very thing that connected us directly to our Creator, and that was our identity. Who we were was directly associated with who God is, but unfortunately, we squandered that relationship for something we thought was better.

It was a vision that Joseph had in Genesis that his brothers would bow down and worship him. At first, this sounded a bit ridiculous to fathom, why would Joseph's older brothers bow down and worship Him? What did Joseph have that they didn't have? Well we find out later in Joseph's story, after being sold into slavery by his own brothers and becoming a prince in Potiphar's house, and then running from the clutches of Potiphar's wife into the confines of a prison cell because of the lies of Potiphar's wife and due to the benevolence of one of Joseph's cellmates, he now has an audience with the King who has been conflicted by a dream. Joseph interprets the dream much to the chagrin of Pharaoh's other hired magicians and soothsayers, and because of God's favor upon the life of Joseph he went from the prison right to the palace. God through the meandering course of Joseph's life fulfilled the vision that Joseph had and his brothers did indeed bow to him as he was now the 2nd in Command in Egypt; 2nd only to Pharaoh himself. What this story reveals is that God-indeed knows what He's doing, and even when things look out of place or out of sorts for us, it is exactly what God has envisioned for us all along.

Is that You?

What is also interesting about this story of Joseph is that his brothers didn't recognize him until Joseph revealed himself to them in Genesis 50:20. It's important to note that here because Joseph revelation was critical, inasmuch as his brothers would not have recognized him on their own. The reason they couldn't recognize Joseph in his new office as the second in command in Egypt, is because they were still preoccupied with seeing Joseph as their little brother. They only saw Joseph as they're little hanger on, or lackey their father Jacob paraded in front of them, because Joseph was his favorite. They restricted their vision of Joseph to just being their little brother and nothing more, which is why his revelation to them took them completely by surprise. There was no way this little peon of a brother could have risen to the be the 2nd in charge in Egypt. Not So! Even though, Joseph had told them of his dreams and vision before they had him sold into Egyptian slavery, but they were too blinded by their jealousy of him to even see the person he would become.

This is an extremely important lesson for us to consider in our pursuit of vision, because God will sometimes remove you from people and places that only have a constricted view of who you are. They can't see your full potential, because they are blinded by the person they want you to be for them. And, there is no future benefit for you continuing to live within the limited framework of someone else's mentality. What benefit is it there for you to continuing living under someone else's narrow perspective of who you are. So, God will essentially free you from that construct in order for you to realize your fullest potential. When this happens then he will bring you back in front of those same people who could only see you for the person they thought you were and not the person God wanted you to be. You are more talented, more gifted, more valuable than they are willing to give you credit for, because they are blinded by what their false perception of you. And, God will move you from those people into a completely different arena where you can thrive and realize your fullest potential, and then bring you back in front of those very same people that could only see you for who they thought you were. Only to show them that you were so much more than they could even fathom. I've often had that happen to me, I would run into an old classmate or an old neighbor friend that I hadn't see in a long time. And, I wouldn't recognize them, because they had change so much over time. Beaten and battered by life, but they would recognize me and the first thing they would say is, "Mike, is that you?" This simple greeting, is yet so profound because you carried the same potential within you when your friends knew you when, but they couldn't see the potential because they could only see you for who they thought you were or who they wanted you to be. This is why, you cannot let people define you, God is the only one that really knows who you are. And, in God's timing He will allow your paths to cross later on down the road, and those same people who couldn't see who you were back then, God will allow them to see you not just for the person you were but for the person you have become.

Ironically, you were always that person they see now, but they were too blinded by who they thought you were to ever see your real potential. A perfect example of this is the caterpillar that slithers up and down a tree branch for weeks and months at time inconspicuously, secretly hiding something immensely beautiful and majestic that the world has never seen before. But, the time isn't yet right for the revelation of what is hidden. However, the day is going to eventually come when the caterpillar is going to go through a complete metabolic metamorphosis, and they will be incubated in a cocoon. And, in this cocoon they are going to undergo a complete and utter transformation from a slithering, inconspicuous mollusk into a gorgeous and majestic butterfly. So, my advice to you is to don't get caught up in how people see you now. You may not have the best-looking clothes, you may not have the best-looking shoes. You may be riding the bus to school or work every day; you may be making minimum wage on a "nickel and dime" job. Don't let where you are today, distract you from reaching your destiny. Don't let how people see you today, influence what you will become tomorrow. Remember, your future and your destiny is not in their hands; tomorrow is not in their hands to decide. You keep your head up, stay focused and determined and don't let who people see with their eyes prevent you from seeing what you will become in your heart. The real "You" is far more valuable than a pair of "Air Jordan's" or "Lebron James." Never let someone devalue your worth based on their limited perspective of who they think you are. My life is meant for far greater, my destiny is meant for so much more.

What is also important to consider is the move-itself; however, on the surface may appear to be purely punitive or diminutive towards you, which sometimes clouds the vision of yourself, and causes feelings of self-pity and anxiety to rise up in you. God moving you from a cantankerous environment may come in the form of a layoff, or a demotion or a firing, and sometimes the malevolence of the move causes you to miss the spiritual insight that it takes a spiritual eye to see. What God meant for a blessing, was viewed as a curse, because you're looking with the wrong eyes at situation with much greater implications. So, we can't continue making superficial judgements based on what we see on the surface, because every move God makes is from a much deeper and more powerful perspective. That's why it is so important for us to see our lives through God's eyes.

What God Sees

What does God see when He looks at me? What causes Him to love me in spite of my constant missteps and misbehaviors? What does God see when He looks at my life; does He see me for the wretch that I am, or does He see someone else? What is God's motivations to love me, when everyone else has given up on me? These are all valid questions, and I'm sure all of us have asked ourselves at one time or another, what was God thinking when He saw me? If we could climb into the mind of God for a short period of time, just so we can examine the answers to these questions carefully, maybe we can understand this merry-go-round we call "life." Knowing what God sees when He looks at me will help me to not only better understand God but will also help me to better understand myself. When God looks at us; I believe, He doesn't immediately see the sinful wretch undone that He ultimately came to save, but actually God sees the person that He saw in the beginning before the world was even formed. He saw my life in the same way He saw it in the beginning as He set down at the drafting board of time and carved out my purpose. How else could a perfect God commune with imperfect man? He does so through the spiritual lens of the future where the beginning meets the ending and vice-versa. This vortex of time is where all of the answers to our spiritual inquiries can be found.

Life would be much simpler if we could just see what God sees for us. If we could just see our lives the way God sees, it would make us all very happy. We probably wouldn't spend as much time murmuring and complaining about the things that we cannot change. Yes, God does see the world for the way it is, but He also able to see our lives not just the way they should be but the way they are going to be. The sad reality is that even though we have the greatest "source" or "resource" in human history, so many still take his presence for granted. If this is indeed an instinctive problem rather than a personality defect then there are other inherent concerns that arise because of this flaw in our humanity. With this reality in mind, we can now see why it is much harder to get a "*BIG*" picture perspective from anyone of us, because we are so inherently consumed by our own reality. Consequently, because of our inherent selfishness we cannot see the interconnectivity or interdependence of our destinies.

It is this interconnectivity and interdependence of the entire world that drives God's agenda for mankind. He is not just concerned about one person or one ethnicity, or one race of people, but He is thoroughly interested in the lives of every single person that He created. God doesn't have the luxury of being selfish; although at the end of the day it is His will that is being accomplished in the life of mankind. So, one could say that He is selfish in a sense, but is it really selfishness, when your will incorporates the lives of every person that was ever created. Or, is it selfishness, when you are not only the Author of your will, but the Finisher of it as well. Is it selfishness when your will contains the interdependence and interconnectivity of everyone's lives in harmonious succession together for the benefit of the greater good. The reality is that we are all walking out the plan and the destiny that God has pre-determined for our lives, and God's plan uniquely includes us all in some way shape or form. We are directly and even indirectly working together to fulfill the plan that God had for us from the very beginning.

What We See

Conversely, when it comes to our vision and our eyesight, it is extremely short-sighted and limited. Although, we are the last to admit it, but what we see is thoroughly wrapped around our selfish self-interests and other self-motivations. Not only are we the last to admit our short-sightedness, we are the first to acknowledge the vastness of what we see. When the depths of the universe secrets are still unknown to us, and yet we arrogantly declare the richness our knowledge and insight that we seem to have. Pride; it seems, is one of our biggest obstacles in truly being able to clearly see what God has in store of us. We are literally, figuratively and even spiritually standing in our own way when it comes to recognizing our limitations and trusting God's capabilities. Herein lies the biggest difference in what we see and what God see's. We can't see God many times, because we are too busy looking at ourselves.

From this perspective; it seems, we are governed heavily by what we see. A lot of weight and stock is put into things that we can see. If we can see it then it must exist. The scientific community puts a slight twist on this analysis, because they concede there are things that we cannot see with our natural eye but do exists. This is why we have telescopes and microscopes to see those things that exists through a more powerful and capable set of lenses. However, where faith and science part ways is when science concludes that anything that cannot be scientifically explained does not exists. Hence their vehement disbelief in the eternal Supreme Being we refer to as God. Not only can God not be seen with natural eyes, but even His existence cannot be explained through scientific measurements. God does not have a beginning or ending, He does not have a birth date that man can figure out. Where is God's DNA for us to analyze and dissect? None of these things exists and yet God still requires for us to believe in Him and reverence Him as the Creator of the heavens and the earth, but for science this is far too much to ask. Their research and the experimentation is what legitimizes this field of study. However, what scientists failed to realize is that everything that they've learned about the universe and the world in which we live is a gift from the God they themselves have problems believing in. The real problem behind scientist's non-belief in a Supreme Being is there is a much stronger belief in themselves. In essence, they have stood in the way of their own divine experience with God, because their quest for knowledge has become their god. Their quest for knowledge has superseded any desire or ambition for a legitimate examination of the ethereal.

God Knows

God knows what's best, and He knows He's the only one that knows what's best, but it is His greatest desire for us to know that about Him from within our hearts; without force or coercion. This is what God essentially wants from you and I. He doesn't want to impose His will upon us, but He wants us to want His will for our lives, because we genuinely know that He knows not only what's best but what's best for us. God's Omniscience or "All Knowing-ness" sets Him apart from everyone else, but not only is He the repository of "All Knowledge" but He is the "Executor" of it is well. No one else's word carries as much weight as God, because of His ability to follow-through on whatever He has decreed. His "All Knowing-ness" works in concert with his "Omnipotence" or "His All Powerful-ness." In that, whatever He decrees, He has the innate ability to bring it to pass. This is why He wants so badly for us to trust His Word over everyone else's for this very reason, He is the only one that is a "Promise keeper" in the truest sense of the term. Mankind because of our limited faculties, intellect, being and otherwise, cannot keep the words that we speak to one another, and yet many times we are more willing to trust the words of one another than the Creator of the heavens and the earth. In essence, we put more confidence in our inabilities than God's abilities, which is absolutely and unequivocally oxymoronic. And, yet we find this to be more of the norm than the anomaly when it comes to having faith in God. We are unwilling; often times, to even give God's will a chance before we elect to do our own thing over what God has planned for our lives. But, why are we so unwilling to give God's plan a chance when there is nothing in His resume that denotes failure. Nothing in God's dossier suggests mistake or error or even accident for that matter, and yet we put more faith and trust in ourselves than we do in Him. Conversely, everything about us screams failure, mistake, and error; in fact, perfection is an impossibility of our existence and yet and still we are more willing to "bet" on ourselves than to simply have faith in a God that never does fail. We seem to be more willing to take a risk on ourselves rather than step out on faith with God, why is that?

Is it because we cannot "*see*" God? Is this the inherent reason why we can't trust God wholeheartedly, because we cannot see Him with our natural eyes? What does seeing God do for our comfort level in trusting Him? The assumption is, how can you trust anyone or anything that you cannot see? However, this is quite easily refuted, because you cannot see the wind, but you see the results of its wrath in moving materials with its weightless might from one area to the next. We cannot see gravity, but we are governed by its invisible rules of engagement, "what goes up must come down." Another example of our blind faith is a simple activity as having a seat, we don't inquire about the architecture of the chair before resting in it. We don't look for the blueprints or the whereabouts of the craftsman to get their perspective on the design of the chair before we sit down it in and yet we blindly sit down believing that the chair's structure can retain our weight without buckling or breaking and we do this continuously and consistently with ever chair we encounter. One might argue that if our blind faith merely resides in a chair we've set in before than maybe this could be the foundation of our confidence or faith, but often times we are blindly resting in places that we never have before and yet our expectations of the outcome are still the same. No one expects the chair to buckle or break, and yet they sometimes do. And, when they do we quickly find another one to sit in, applying our blind faith to yet another untested untried object that we know very little about. I am in no way equating our relationship with God and challenges with having faith to the inane activity of sitting in a chair. It is just a simple observation that provides some insight into our natural proclivities when it comes to things we see and things we can't see.

Vision Takes Patience

While working on a " DIY project with my wife, I was struck with a revelation about vision that I had to share in this chapter. When tackling a big DIY project at home it is easy to get overwhelmed by the size of it, in fact it is easy to get intimidated by the size of, which may cause you to completely forfeit the endeavor altogether. For me, when working on big projects at home several questions pop into my mind that helps me to judge whether this is an achievable goal or should we pass this on to the professionals. The first question I ask is "have we given ourselves enough time to complete this project?" Often these projects are initiated by some event we are having and as a part of sprucing up the old homestead we begin to tackle a DIY that might enhance the event even more. However, we haven't given ourselves enough time to complete the project before the date of the event we're supposed to be hosting. So, we start wrong and what usually starts wrong ends wrong, or it takes even more effort to get right before the blessed event.

Likewise, with vision, we have to understand that visions are usually long-term goals that are going to take time for them to be achieved. The worst thing that we can do is rush the timing of a vision, because we want it before God is ready for us to have it. We must always remember that God's timing is different from our timing. In fact, His way of doing things is much different than our way of doing things. And, just as the song writer said,

You can't hurry God, you just have to wait.
You have to trust Him and give Him, no matter how long it takes.
He's a God you just can't hurry.

He'll be there don't you worry.
He may not come when you want Him but He's right on time.

Vision takes patience. In other words, anything that involves God takes patience. He is not one to rush his will for our lives. He has an appointed time for us and we have to wait until He's ready, before we can receive whatever He has for our lives.

Another interesting part about DIY projects is that you can easily get overwhelmed by the size of the project, which may cause you to give up even before you start. It can also cause you to have a defeated attitude all while trying to complete it, because your mind is completely intimidated by the size of the project. So, what is helpful in these situations is to break the project down into "bit-sized" compartments where you able to see the small accomplishments, which will ultimately lead to bigger ones if you continue to stay focus on your goal. However, as you are working if your focus strays back towards the size of the project it can negatively impact your attitude, which will impact your willingness to continue because of how insurmountable this project seems to be.

As it relates to vision, it is in our minds eye that drives the perception of our natural eye. Inasmuch, as we are comparing the size of the vision to the person we are now and weighing that against our ability to complete whatever the vision was that we saw. But, we must remember that God is going to help us to reach this goal, so we shouldn't overly concern ourselves with the particulars, just as long as we know God is the one that is going to make it all happen in the end. This is another reason why He doesn't give it all to us at once anyway, because He knows we couldn't handle it. God, many times, metes out our vision in small doses, because He knows if He gave it to us all at once it would overwhelm us. If He gave it to us all at once it would probably destroy us, so God in His infinite wisdom, decides when and what He wants to share with us about the vision He has for our lives. It is an extraordinary undertaking, which should give you some idea of the awesome expectations that God has for us. Just as our introductory quote declares, Jeremiah in 29:11 (KJV) when He says, "For I know the thoughts that I think towards you saith God, thoughts of peace and not of evil, to give you an expected end." God thoughts of us are good; not evil ones. He is not thinking evil thoughts about us, which is also not "why" we may be experiencing some difficulties in our lives. Our problems do not exist, because God is thinking evil thoughts for us. God wants us to succeed, He only wants the best for us. This scripture unequivocally proves that. He wants nothing but the best for us. The problem comes when we try to get ahead of God, and out think Him and His plan for our lives. Our lack of patience will sometimes cause us to jump out ahead of God, because His timing seems to be so out of sync with ours. We must remember that He alone has the power to make our dreams a reality, and we have to trust in not only His ability but also His timing.

Sometimes it is our mind that causes us to want to interfere with God's timing. We're are trying to process the series of events that will lead up to our pending success, and it seems like God is taking longer than we think He should to get us there. Our impatience has cause more trouble for people than I can even imagine. And, in this midst of this waiting period, we let our negative thoughts overwhelm us, and anxiety over take us, and we allow what we see mentally to govern our entire well-being. That is a dangerous space to be in, especially when your perception of things is completely false. We don't realize how powerful our minds are as it relates to the impact of positive or negative thoughts. We have the freedom as well as the power to think positively and negatively in our minds, and whatever the outcome could be attributed to the influence of those thoughts. Our thoughts are powerful enough to control our attitude and behavior, and if they are powerful enough to control our attitude and our behavior they are also powerful enough to control our actions as well. The Bible says, in Proverbs 23:7, (KJV) "as a man thinketh in his heart, so is he." So, we have been given a great deal of mental power that can ultimately determine how we function naturally. If we chose to look at a situation negatively, then no matter how others might try to change our thinking or our perception of the situation, if we don't choose to change our perception than our perception won't change. It works the same way positively, but it is essentially based on our volition to cooperate with the competing perceptions of our reality, if are original state of mind will change or not. No one can change our thoughts for us. We have to change them ourselves. We have to see value in being positive, speaking positive, thinking positive, over becoming overwhelmed by negativity, before our mindset will ever change. In the final analysis, the decision is entirely up to us in whom we are going to ultimately place our trust, are we going to trust God and what He sees for our life and be blessed, or are we going to continue trusting our limited vision and what we see and be cursed? The choice is up to you!

CHAPTER 4

OUR VISION

"The greatest danger for most of us is not that our aim is too high and we miss it, but that it is too low and we reach it."

- Michelango

Our vision sometimes is reflective of our environment; where and how we were raised, what school we attended, how was our family life, were there two parents in the home, did we have any siblings, did we attend church, these are just a few of the scenarios that helps to shape the vision we have for ourselves. All of these factors play an extremely important role in ultimately shaping our outlook on life. There is no cookie cutter answer to any of these questions, in fact the answers are going to be inevitably different, primarily because we all have different life experiences and it is from these life experiences that our outlook on life is shaped. This is why a young inquisitive entrepreneur started a website; years ago, for college students to study and to share experiences online and has now become one of the world's leading social media outlets. I have met very few people who dint have at least one Facebook page, so we can see that this platform is extremely far-reaching. Or how a young high-school student from North Carolina who got cut from his high school basketball team refused to allow that to be the conclusion to "his-story." But, instead chose to make history by continuing to work on his game competing against his older brother, excelling at the collegiate level at University of North Carolina; where he is still "thee" most famous Tar-Heel, drafted by the Chicago Bulls and would become arguably the greatest basketball players to ever play the game. These success stories did not begin nor end with other people's perception of them, but it is based on how they perceive themselves. Yes, they faced adversity, and some of the answers to our earlier questions I'm sure were of a negative sort, but it did not deter them from reaching their ultimate goals of pursuing their life's dreams. The answers to our earlier questions can positively or negatively affect the way you see the world around you, the way you see others and ultimately how you see yourself. The challenge for every person living and breathing is to never allow what you've been through to keep you from where you want to go.

Our vision can sometimes get weighted down with the harsh realities of life that serve as constant reminders of the everyday obstacles we may face. Our impoverished upbringing, dilapidated housing, inferior schools, crime infested neighborhoods are the realities of a whole host of young people that have ironically been called our future. Society says that the majority of these youth will either end up in prison or dead before they reached their 18th birthday. However, these statistics does not have to be your reality; these predictions do not have to be your future. In fact, we hear of a countless number of success stories who testify had it not been for their meager upbringing; had it not been for the odds that were exponentially stacked against them; had it not been for the tremendous pressure of complacency lorded over them, they wouldn't have the drive nor the motivation to succeed.

I Am the Captain of My Fate

What we discover as we get older and more mature is that success usually begins from a place of obscurity. Potential usually comes from a place of hopelessness. I know it sounds strange, but as you review the lives of the many men and women who successes and failures have been recorded by history you will find that most of them came from a place of obscurity; a place of darkness; an obscene place, but the great thing about their story is that it didn't end there. On the surface, everything about their neighborhood said failure; on the surface, everything about their schools said dropout; on the surface, everything about their future said hopeless. Subsequently, this is why you can't regulate your sight to only what you see on the surface, because although the surface looks like concrete the ground is still fertile enough to grow a beautiful rose. Your sight has to encompass more than what you visualize with your natural eyes, but you've got to look deeper than what you see on the surface. One thing to remember in this pursuit of fulfillment, obscurity is only the beginning, notoriety is your final-destination. They may not know who you are now, but you keep working, you keep grinding, you keep dreaming, you keep seeing and one day they will recognize you in a crowded auditorium. You may not have had any say in how your story began, but you do have the power to determine how your story will end.

Author and poet Willian Ernest Henley wrote the famous poem "Invictus" which I believe captures the spirit of every would be visionary;

Out of the night that covers me,
Black as the Pit from pole to pole,
I thank whatever gods may be
For my unconquerable soul,

In the fell clutch of circumstance
I have not winced nor cried aloud,
Under the bludgeoning of chance
My head is bloody, but unbowed.

Beyond this place of wrath and tears
Looms but the Horror of the shade,
And yet the menace of the years
Finds, and shall find me unafraid

It matters not how strait the gate
How charged with punishments the school
I am the master of my fate:
I am the captain of my soul

Some tend to focus on the sheer arrogance of the last stanza where he declares, "I am the master of my fate, I am the captain of my soul," and scoff at the audacity of this language. How can one be so unilateral in their thinking when it comes to disseminating their fate when there are so many other factors at play most of which you cannot humanly control. However, it is the spirit of the poem that I would like to emphasize for in it we cannot help but see a determination and a tenacity that is extraordinary. And that is the kind of determination and tenacity that every visionary needs in order to be successful in life.

Sometimes our vision is clouded by things we see. This statement might seem a bit oxymoronic, but is very much a true statement. Our vision can become clouded by the negative things that we see around us that can keep us from reaching our fullest potential. The obstacles we see in our way become bigger and more obtuse the more prominence we give to them in our everyday lives. In life, we all are going to face some challenges, but how you chose to deal with them is what makes one a success and the other a failure. In other words, our problems are the litmus test of our success or failure, are you going to choose to be defined by them or are you going to defy them and become better. Every successful person had to decide at one time or another am I going to allow my problems to limit my perception of myself or am I going to use my problems as my motivation to succeed.

We cannot allow our vision to become so clouded by the machinations of today that you cannot even see a brighter tomorrow. This is a very dangerous place to be, when you have reached a point of hopelessness. What is unfortunate is that there are so many people that find themselves in this dangerous self-defeating state of mind. You cannot be a forward thinker when you are hopeless; you cannot be optimistic when you have a hopeless disposition. This self-defeating spirit has ended many a life, simply because they seem to be too preoccupied with today to ever consider if there will ever be tomorrow.

The Miseducation of Billy Watts

Our society is littered with stories of people who have given up on family, friends, neighbors, and most importantly themselves. I'm reminded of a fairly recent story of a young high school student by the name of Billy Watts aka "DJ Kill Bill" who committed suicide back in Oct of 2014 by jumping into the Detroit River. As if his mere suicide isn't bad enough, he carefully and meticulously planned out his own death via his Instagram feed. The final days and even moments leading up to his eventual demise were chronicled on his personal Instagram account. Everything from a photo of his last hair cut to a picture of his final meal. There is even a last photo of him smiling into the camera as he stands in front of what would end up being his final resting place. According to news outlets that reported on this story Billy Watts; who had been battling depression for many months before his untimely death, drowned himself in the Detroit River. The extremely sad part about his story is that no one seemed to care; at least until it was absolutely too late. You see adding the component of social media to his decision to commit suicide opened up the door for the entire Internet to get an up-close and personal look at his own demise. People were posting comments under each picture some before and many others after this young man plunged to his death in the Detroit River. What is interesting is the level of concern many seemed to have for this young man after the fact, when it was blatantly obvious that he needed someone who was concerned about his well-being before that fateful day in October. But, maybe this is what Billy wanted, maybe he wanted people to feel the void of his absence, much in the same way he probably felt overlooked while in their presence. Maybe Billy felt the only way that he could truly be remembered is if he was truly gone. These are all mere speculations about the promising life of a young man that ended too soon.

Billy Watts story is not unlike many others who because of a bout with depression decided to take their own life. Believing that somehow, they are relieving themselves of their problems, when in reality they have only made matters much worst. How could one's vision become so blurred that the only rational way to resolve this is to take your own life. I remember sharing his story with the students at my church and the many different responses we got from them about this disturbed young man. In fact, one of the students was actually good friends with Billy before he took his life and it was expressed that he never let on that he was suffering with depression, and nobody knew except his thousands of Instagram followers what his plans were or maybe they too didn't have a clue

For someone like Billy who was dealing with severe depression there had to be some tell-tale signs that he was going through something that if only someone could have picked up on it might have saved his life. After just looking at his Instagram account and seeing some of his photos, it was enough for me to see that this young man was severely disturbed. In one photo, there was a picture of a woman at the bottom of the ocean floor with a broken neck and another photo of the "Eye of Horus" a very popular Satanic occult symbol. Another very telling sign to me that something was very wrong with this young man was the found in the name he was known to many of his classmates as well as followers on social media as "DJ Kill

Bill," a deejaying name he chose for himself that oddly enough reflected the future he planned for himself. If this isn't one of the most blatant and overt signs that something is wrong, I'm not sure what is. Yet another very important insight into the disturbing psyche of this depressed young man. And in some ways, those who called him by his nickname were involuntary accessories in his own demise. Every time they called him "DJ Kill Bill" they could have very well been reaffirming his own self-destructive plans. This is why names are so very important. What you name yourself or what you name your children are extremely important, because sometimes our limited vision of not just ourselves but even our offspring is contained in the name that we give them. Sheniqua, Mercedes, Blue Ivy, North, Apple, or Peaches are just a few of the given names by parents who obviously lacked the foresight and vision for their own children to handicap them from birth with a name so demeaning and short-sighted. "Apple" is the name of Gwyneth Paltrow and Coldplay front man Chris Martin's daughter. And her explanation for her name choice was "Apples are so sweet, and they're wholesome, and it's biblical — and I just thought it sounded so lovely and ... clean!" One can only imagine the mental and psychological damage that this name will eventually cause this child as she grows up being picked on and teased by classmates about her unusual name. Some will probably say that because Gwyneth Paltrow is rich and because she's a celebrity this will shield her daughter from the negative climate that other lesser privileged children may grow up in. And, in part they may be true, but that still is no excuse for giving the fruit of your lions the same name as a fruit.

A Rose by Any Other Name

What we failed to realize is our positive or negative self-image is often derived from what we are called. This is why great time and attention should be taken when determining the names of our children. First and foremost, these will be the names that will follow them throughout their entire lives. We also can limit our offspring socioeconomically by giving them names that restrains them to a certain socioeconomic class of people. Naming your child "Peaches" or "Apple" you might as well fit them for their "Red-light District" uniform; if you don't have the means or the resources to redirect their career choices. Hopefully you get my point, what you name your child directly and indirectly coincides with the expectations that you have for them. And, your expectations quickly become society's expectations of them as well, simply by what you call them. Of course, there are exceptions to ever rule, who would've thought that the name Barack Hussein Obama would be the name of the 44th President of these United States. This is not your typical presidential name, I mean we are used to hearing names like George Herbert Walker Bush, William Jefferson Clinton, and John Fitzgerald Kennedy. Barack Obama is indeed an anomaly, so is the name Donald Trump but for far more dark and sinister reasons. President Obama said the same of himself and coupled with his sordid background that he was born out of, he could have certainly succumbed to the pressures of environment but he decided to do something different. His life seems to always reflect a quest or search for something better or something more, not just for himself but for everybody else.

Names are just one component of all of this and it is not our intention to exaggerate this point to implicitly or even explicitly suggests that our successes and failures solely lie within the convention of our names, but it is definitely a good place to start. In William Shakespeare's play "Romeo and Juliet" there is a famous quote by Juliet while trying to convince Romeo that it does not matter that he is from her rival house of Montague, she proclaimed "a rose by any other name would smell would smell just as sweet." In other words, who you are is much more important than what you have been called or where you are from. I often use the advice that I was given as a child when being picked on and teased by other kids, "it's not what you're called, it's what you answer to!" And, yes you can be a success with an unconventional name, it has been done before and will continue. We have the Oprah's, the Obamas, the Lebron's, and many others that can attests to this, their success did not come from their name but it is certainly tied to their name. There's a difference.

This is all apart of our vision, which is connected directly to our lateral perception of ourselves and the world around us. Our names, our environment, our family and friends, our schools, churches and other social networks, are all some of the external components that help to shape the physical, mental and even spiritual perception of ourselves. These external components are the things on the outside that we interact with on a regular basis that help to shape our mental perception of self. The environment where we grew up, our neighbors and friends within that community could be considered the people that help us to understand the world around us. How your family, friends and neighbors viewed the world ultimately effects the way you will see it yourself.

What's in Front of You

Our vision is primarily horizontal, which means we are usually more focused on the things which are in front of us, and that includes material as well as immaterial things, i.e. car, house, family, bills, finances, job, relationships, etc. These are the things that preoccupy and occupy our thinking. Our horizontal vision is what takes up most of our time, looking at and dealing with things that are directly or indirectly in front of us. And, it is this horizontal vision that get us into trouble many times, because as we become so inundated with what is in front of us, we cannot see any further than that, and this is when our vision becomes short-sighted. Horizontal vision encompasses both the physical and the mental, because the two works inter-dependently of one another. Your mental perception is directly tied to what you physically see, and your physical sight directly effects your mental perception; the two go hand in hand. I am a very analytical person, some might say too analytical at times. So, my brain is constantly processing the things that I physically see. In fact, one of my favorite past times is to go to the mall or sit outside a public place and just people watch. You can learn a lot watching other people. Being observant is one very important component of success that I learned at a very young age. Sometimes you can save yourself a world of trouble, by watching other people get in to trouble. You know there are two kinds of people, people who learn by experience, and people who learn from other people's experiences. I am more of the second kind, primarily because I would much rather observe and watch before I step out and do anything. From this standpoint, you are able to learn from someone else's mistakes and failures on what not to do in order to get more positive results. Some might say this "cherry picking" or "living too cautiously" but there is virtue and extremely high value in watching and observing other people before you endeavor to do any of the same things. To those who say that a person who is too observant is "cherry picking" their way through life, in other words they are saying you are not willing to take risks, which can get you further ahead if you are willing to step outside of your comfort zone a bit. There is nothing wrong with taking risks, and yes, in life you will have to take some risks, you will have to give caution to the wind and step out there without a life preserver and sink or swim.

However, I believe there is a wealth of knowledge that comes from observing those who had success as well as failures. In fact, I believe you can learn more from someone's mistakes than their successes, simply because knowing "what not to do" is just as important if not more than knowing what to do. And, there seems to be so many creative ways not to do something that you will be selling yourself short to not sit back and take notes watching someone make the mistakes before you did. This might seem a bit selfish in thinking, but I find it even more disturbing when you watch someone repeat the same behavior of another person that ultimately led them down a wrong path and if they only had the wisdom or the presence of mind to be more observant they could have seen a head of time the destruction that was coming by watching someone else, then to have not seen it and ended up in the same unfortunate circumstances as the first person. I was never the kind of child that learned from experience. When my mother told me not to touch the stove because it was hot, I found more value in listening to her instruction rather than learning through my disobedience that the stove was just as hot as my mother had already said. And, with my disobedience comes the consequence of having a burnt hand, which could have very well been avoided had I simply listened to my mother's original instructions.

Conversely, there are those who still chose to; after having been given a verbal warning not to do something, still step out and attempt the very same thing they were told not to. Why is that? Is it something in their psyche that is telling them that they are ultimately being restricted or limited to only do a certain thing, essentially because someone told them they couldn't. This authoritarian type of discipline is stifling to the born risk takers of our society. On one hand, we can see how this authoritarian approach would cause some children to rebel, because they instinctively are attracted to what is taboo or forbidden. This is why parents have to constantly tell their small children not to touch electrical outlets, and to stay away from things that are hot, because they are trying to prevent them from experiencing the negative consequences of their actions. However, on the other hand, in a completely different scenario we can see how this authoritarian approach might ignite some risk takers to do what others said is absolutely impossible. Sometimes, hearing "that you can't do something" is all the incentive a risk taker needs to at least try what others deem to be ridiculous. This explains why a 70-year-old woman would jump out of an airplane at 30,000 feet in the air sky diving, because her family told her it was an extraordinarily difficult thing for a person her age to try to do.

This is a fairly extreme example of this, but we heard it said before that "crime doesn't pay." Yet, we do find that there are so many curious people out there they actually want to see if that's a true statement or not? We know crime doesn't pay, and yet we see and hear in the news everyday where there are criminals out there testing the merits of this statement. Go figure!

Peace and Piece

Our vision is flawed; our vision is imperfect; our vision is skewed, our vision is distorted, our vision is short-sighted, our vision is limited, and for these reasons and many more we need God's vision in order to see clearly. It is through God's eyes that our life's trials and tribulations makes sense; it is through His microscopic lenses that tumultuous ups and downs of this life serves a greater purpose. This is why spiritual vision transcends the physical and mental, because it offers a new perspective on life that hasn't been revealed in the other two. Spiritual vision allows you to look at the same problem that you've viewed both naturally and perceived mentally and see a solution when initially you only saw the problem. We spoke of our vision being horizontal, which means that we typically deal with things that are immediately in front of us. God's vision, on the other hand is vertical, which means you can see life from an entirely new and different perspective. With God's vision, you are able to see life as it was meant to be. You can appreciate the splendor of God's creation, you can see purpose intermingled into everything that God made. And, purpose is the missing piece or peace; whichever one you want to use, in many of our lives. Purpose is the missing piece that can help us to understand the direction our life has taken. Purpose is the missing piece that we need for our life to make sense. Purpose is the vehicle that God used to create the world and everything in it, and you can't live your life without it.

Many have tried and many have failed. And, peace comes in understanding that my life has a purpose. God's vision brings a peace, according to Philippians 4:17 (KJV) "that passeth all understanding." When everyone is falling apart, because you understand that purpose is bigger than my problems, you have entered a realm of peace that everyone cannot enter. When you can see your life through the lens of purpose you now have peace. You have peace, because you know that no matter what happens to me, no matter what problems I experience; it's all for a purpose. A purpose that I might not understand right now; a purpose that might not be completely clear right now, but there is a divine reason behind it. The reason might be above my pay grade right now, but when the time is right God will reveal to me the who, what, when, where and the how. The key to having real peace is being able to trust that His eyes are much better than mine. Real peace comes when you understand that God sees what you can't see, and because of Him having this divine perspective my life now makes sense. Having this knowledge of His divine perspective makes my life have more meaning and value. This; however, is not a guarantee that He will always show us what He sees. Sometimes, it is the experience that He wants for us to have before the purpose of it is revealed. Here is yet another "*P*" word that is another missing piece for so many of us and that is patience. We have to trust in His divine perspective and believe that God's eyes are better than ours.

The Psychology of Slavery

The quote from Michelango for this chapter is so apropos, when it comes to our vision it is not that our aim is too high and we miss it, it is that it's too low and we reach it. There seems to be a satisfaction with mediocrity that is sublime; a fascination with being average that is mind-boggling. Where did this come from? Why do we only reach for things that we know are within our grasp? Why don't we strive for anything more? It seems that our expectations have become aligned with what we see, and when this happens we have stumbled upon a valley of complacency that has severely affected the way see ourselves, our lives and our future. We see death so we expect to die, we see violence, so we become violent, we see poverty so we become impoverished, we see negativity, so we become pessimistic. This happens when our physical environments become our mental and psychological prisons. People who cannot see their future because they are mental prisoners of their today. And, the interesting thing about prison is that you don't have to be locked up to be in prison. You don't have to be in physical chains to be in bondage or slavery. In fact, the most dangerous as well as effective kind of slavery is mental slavery. This transcends any physical chains or bondage anyone could ever submit to. When there are chains placed on your mind, the physical chains can be removed and you will still behave like a slave, because your mind is the epicenter of your thoughts. And, this is where slavery was its most impactful, inasmuch as even when the slaves were given their physical freedom they still remained slaves because the very thing they needed to survive was locked up in a mental prison.

You've ever been around mediocre thinkers? You've ever been around people who can only see themselves in a certain reality, because this has been there reality for so long that they feel nothing more is possible. I remember my first job as stock boy at K-Mart, and I remember being excited to have a job and to be able to earn my own money. It was a part-time job and I only worked a few hours a week; just enough money to keep me going while I was in my last year of high school and headed into my first year of college. I started this job with a great deal of optimism and independence, because now I was able to take care of myself in a way that I never could before. And, I remember my shift was the evening shift which begin about 5:00 and it would briefly overlap the out-going full-time employees whose shifts were just ending as mine was just getting started. And, I remember sitting back in the break room listening to the older men talk about their jobs as if they were in some kind of prison facility. They're talking about the boss like he's a slave master and they are field slaves whose shift for the days is coming to an end and this was their opportunity to educate the young rookies who were picking up where they left off. Their attitudes were negative and complacent, and you could tell by their conversation that K-Mart had taken up a lot of mental real estate. Men who had worked there 30 or 40yrs; ready to retire, who may very well have started this job with a similar mindset as mine but over time became trapped by their environment and could no longer see a way out. Now they have taken on the vernacular of their environment, and essentially become a living, breathing reflection of the place that had imprisoned their thinking. I, on the other hand was treating this job as a stop on my way to my destination; I had much bigger plans than becoming a career stock-boy at K-Mart. My goal at the time was to go to Michigan State University major in Political Science and go to law school and practice law. So, K-Mart was never intended to be my destination.

Any place that has become your destination is also your destiny. This is why you have to expand your thinking; expand your paradigm when it comes to you and your future. The prayer of Jabazz was to enlarge his territory. The larger your vision becomes, the greater the territory you were assigned to conqueror. So, whatever happened there for the few hours I was working as a stock boy stayed there. I didn't bring anything from that job home with me, because there was nothing within those walls important enough for me to allow to take up valuable mental real estate. I treated the job just like that was all it was. I had a great work ethic, which I got from my father; there was a commitment and dedication that was intertwined into his work ethic that quickly became a part of my DNA once I became gainfully employed. So, the dynamic of my interaction with those who were fully vested into mental slavery at K-Mart, and me being someone who; while I appreciated having a job, never saw it as anything more than a stop gap to something much, much better. I would take what they would say to me in passing with a grain of salt, but never would I allow it to take up full residence in my mind. You can't allow small things to take up so much space in your mind. This is the equivalent of eagles hanging around chickens. The longer you hang around chickens, the more of their characteristics you will start to adopt. And, this is essentially what is happening when we settle for mediocrity; we implicitly suggest through the process of settling that we are satisfied being a third of ourselves instead of working at full capacity.

Don't Settle

The best advice that I can give in this book is to never be satisfied, stay hungry, stay motivated, stay inspired to be the best version of yourself that you can be. One of the greatest enemies of vision is settling. When you settle you are essentially saying that "I refuse to try" "I am completely satisfied being right where I am." There is no greater enemy to progress than complacency and stagnation. You cannot go anywhere standing still. You were created to be more, to do more; there is much more value and potential in you if you just take the time to look. There should always be that desire, that compulsion to do better than you did before, to stretch yourself beyond what you did previously, to continue to challenge yourself to be the best "you" possible. This is the mantra of successful people, they are never satisfied with what they did yesterday, they are constantly trying to find ways to improve and get better. When you lose that desire you are in a world of trouble. Why? Because, your gift and talents are not for you but they are for the world that you live in and if you refuse to share them with the world then what kind of impact will they essentially have? There are people waiting on the very thing that you have to offer; there are people that God created specifically to be beneficiaries of your gift. What will happen to them if they never experience your presence? What will become of them? What you don't realize is that their purpose was to be inspired through the fulfillment of your purpose. Dr. King pointedly declared, "our destinies are inextricably tied to one another" in other words, we all are cosmically connected to one another, we are all a part of the economy of the world, which ultimately impacts everyone whether it be directly or indirectly. With this concept in mind, what I do or don't do does matter, it does make a difference, it is impactful to the whole of mankind. This statement clearly puts our purpose in its proper perspective, we are not here just for ourselves, but we are here to help our fellow man. What God has given you, He didn't give it to anyone else, what He has for you to do, you are the only one assigned to do it. So, it is incumbent upon you to fulfill your purpose, stretch yourself to your fullest potential. Don't let anything or anybody deter you from being the best "you" that you can be. Someone is depending on your vision, someone is waiting on what you've been dreaming about, the world is waiting with bated breath for the real you to emerge. The question is will you continue to keep them waiting, vacillating between two opinions; or will you rise to the occasion and become what the worlds been waiting for?

Your Own Worst Enemy

Have you heard the phrase, we have become our own worst enemy? In other words, it is not the enemy on the outside that does us the most harm, but many times it is in the enemy within that is our greatest adversary. A very telling statement about the internal battles that we face, which keep us from reaching our fullest potential. One would assume that if we have goal in front of us that we would put forth our best effort in trying to achieve it, and would not in any way; whether it be intentional or unintentional, stand in the way of fulfilling said goal. However, according to this statement we can stand in our own way when it comes to accomplishing goals we've set for ourselves. This seems a bit oxymoronic. Why would I want to stand in my own way, when these are my goals that I want to accomplish.

But, it is true we can ultimately be the only thing standing in the way of our success, primarily because of fear, lack of faith, skewed or distorted vision. These along with many other obstacles can contribute to the internal struggle for success that we will ultimately encounter with ourselves. We are consciously and even subconsciously prepared for the interruption or interference from an outside adversary or foe as it relates to achieving goals. In fact, this is something we've probably heard ad nausea that whenever you plan to do something, plan to encounter some haters or adversaries that don't want to see you make it. We've come to expect some friction from the "haters" who spend their time trying to stop us from achieving our goals. And, of course we've heard the motivational speeches and the sermons that characterize the "haters" as people who are constantly chasing you, and why should you ever look back to entertain people that are trying to stop you. Or, we've heard the size of your haters is often times an indication of the size of the goal you're trying to achieve. Conversely, if you don't have any haters than you must not be doing anything worthwhile. Or, you don't have any haters than you must not be that gifted. These are usually what we hear when it comes to the external adversary that comes to stop you, but what about the internal foe that resides within your own subconscious mind that has come to discourage you, depress you, overwhelm you to the point of never pursuing your dreams at all. We have been pre-conditioned to look outside of ourselves for our next enemy, but what about the enemy within. You mean to tell me that there is an enemy within me that can work equally as hard to stop me, as I am to pursue my dreams and visions? Yes, there certainly is. Doubt, fear, anxiety, are some of the internal dream killers that will cloud you mind with so much negativity that if you don't have some positive reinforcement to combat the overwhelming negativity you will want to stop yourself. This is why it is so important that you do whatever is necessary to stay inspired, empowered and motivated to achieve your goals. Read empowering and inspiring books, listen to powerful motivational speeches and sermons, find a mentor to shadow, or spend time encouraging yourself and reminding yourself of the goals you've already accomplished. You have to continue to feed the desire to succeed within you, because the more that you feed this desire with positive thinking the greater its presence will be within your own subconscious. The more powerful it will be against those competing thoughts of doubt, fear and anxiety that are constantly pushing you to give up. A great man once said, "if there is no enemy within, the enemy outside can do you no harm." In other words, if there is nothing stopping you on the inside, then won't anything be able to stop you on the outside. The drive pushing you has got to be exponentially stronger than the internal thoughts trying to stop you. Whichever force is the strongest is usually the one that ultimately wins in the end. You have the power within to you to succeed. Never allow those internal thoughts to overwhelm your drive for greatness.

Chapter 5

DISTRACTED VISION

"You can't do big things if you are distracted by small things"
— African Proverb

Imagine if the greatest men and women that history has ever recorded, instead of them being great leaders, singers, speakers, politicians, scholars, scientists, engineers, entertainers, inventors and the like, they succumb to the plethora of distractions that often hindered their creativity. Not only would they have not excelled at the highest level in their respective professions, but the entire world would not have benefited from their genius. The impact of their absence in our world would far exceed their own individual disappointments for not fulfilling the vision and dreams they had for themselves. This is the power of distraction, because its impact can be utterly diabolical if you allow it to overwhelm you and interrupt your drive to move forward. The power of distraction can be a completely destructive force, because with it comes the annihilation of any future aspirations that one might have because their attention has been diverted elsewhere. Most times elsewhere it's not another place of productivity, it is not a place of creativity, but instead if it is a place of "*do* nothingness," laziness and idleness.

My Dirty Little Secret

If there is one criticism I have of myself and that is that I watch far too much television. I'm sure I'm not alone in this admission, but if we are all honest with ourselves, the time that we devote to essentially watching other people be successful at whatever craft they have on display for that brief moment they have our attention could very well have been used for more productive pursuits. I'm certainly guilty of spending too much time in front of the television. Time wasted, watching other people maximize their talents and abilities, whether we like what we're watching or not, by virtue of us watching someone other than ourselves they have achieved a level of success that we haven't because we are watching them and they are not watching us. When you think about the countless hours that you spend in front of the TV, and TVs have evolved and they are much more advanced and sophisticated than the obtuse wide bodied antiquated cathode ray tubes they were thirty or forty years ago. It seems technology in some ways has become an accomplice to our inactivity and stagnation, because as it advances we seem to be standing still mesmerized by the twenty-first century conveyances of modern technology. Our personal goals never seem to advance as fast as the technology that has captivated our attention with such things like Flat Screen TVs, 3D & 4K TVs, surround sound, bigger and more clearer screens, Blu-ray disc players, and other home theatre type amenities. These things are real-life distractions if we allow them to control our lives. We cannot allow these superficial accouchements to become our ultimate creative demise, because we are caught up in self-indulgence rather than self –improvement. It is important that we maintain a healthy balance between entertainment and self-improvement, because both are needed in ordered to be a well-adjusted individual.

"A new study, published today in Journal of the American Heart Association, found that adults who watch TV three hours or more a day may be twice as likely to die prematurely than those who watch an hour or less."

These are extremely alarming statistics that Nielsen has calculated concerning American's addiction to television. Five hours a day of productivity wasted watching someone else be productive. America's love affair with television has brought us quite some ways, and we must thank a whole host of actors, actresses, producers, directors, TV execs and the like for providing us with weekly entertainment that we can use to unwind and relax. However, if we use even a small modicum of that time each day to do something productive our lives would be much better for it. We need to spend more time working on ourselves and improving ourselves so that we can walk into greater opportunities. Life is about constant preparation for that next opportunity. My favorite quote by Whitney M. Young is, "It is better to be prepared for an opportunity and not have one than to have an opportunity and not be prepared." So, our entire lives should be spent in preparation for an opportunity that has not materialized yet. Life is a dress rehearsal for the performance of a lifetime. We must use these saying to help to keep us motivated and to properly put into perspective the value of time. We were not created to waste time. Time is a fleeting mechanism that no one is promised a certain amount of, so we must glean from it the value that it brings. The Bible speaks of "redeeming the times," because there is no one that understands the value of time better than the Creator of it. Since we were all created on purpose with a purpose, we should easily conclude that someone thought enough of you to not only create you, but He gave each one of us something to do.

When you think about the impact of being distracted and the enormous time that is wasted being unproductive and lazy, the results are staggering. You can usually mete out success by what was accomplished, what goals were achieved, what was done, these are measurable's that can be used to evaluate your effectiveness.

Can You Afford to Be Distracted?

Can you afford to be distracted? This is an obviously loaded question for several reasons, firstly because it is a question directly related to time. If time is in fact a fleeting mechanism and if it's true the more time we have the more time we waste, then it really does beg the question "can we really afford to waste time?" Secondly, what is also inferred with this question is value, because being able to afford something insinuates a "cost" associated with it. And, so if the cost which is the act of being distracted is greater than the value of what it is you're trying to accomplish than maybe what you're doing isn't really all that important. Conversely, if the value of what you are attempting to accomplish is greater than the cost of being distracted then the answer to our initial question of can you afford to be distracted is an emphatic NO. When you think about the amount of time that is wasted every day and when you compare that to the hours of productivity that we use toward being productive, many of us are professional "time wasters." There should be a sense of urgency with everything that we do. This; I believe, is a key difference between success and failure. The successful already have the mindset that time is not a commodity that they can afford to waste. In fact, they equate their time on the same level as their money. I'm sure you've heard it said before, "time is money." Maybe time is more important than money, because at least with money if you do lose some; which is a reality we all must face, we can certainly work to get it back. However, once time is gone it is gone never to return. Therefore, not wasting time is critically important, because the purpose God has for us is not just designed for our benefit but it is specifically designed for somebody else. What God wants to do through you is really to help somebody else. The vision that God has given you is not for you, but the real purpose, the real objective is for you to fulfill a need that someone else has in their life. Vision in this sense becomes exponentially important, because it wasn't essentially given to us to benefit us, but when God saw us operating in our purpose it was to benefit another group of people. So, if we get distracted and lose focus and do not fulfill the purpose that God has for us than what about those people that our vision was designed to impact? What becomes of those that you were essentially created to save? This truly puts the impact of purpose and vision into proper perspective, because when we typically discuss purpose and vision we do so from a ratio of 1:1, in other words what I do only affects me; my vision, my goals will only impact me, which is an extremely selfish perspective, and quite erroneous to say the least. Nothing that we do in life only impacts or affects us, but it impacts or affects the life of someone else whether directly or indirectly. In an earlier chapter, we briefly talked about the interconnectivity and interdependence of mankind as a whole. How we are all tied together in a single garment of destiny, which should put the reality of our decisions in their proper perspective. For the sake of mankind, we can ill afford to take a selfish perspective when it comes to helping to improve the lives of others through the vision that God gave to us. We cannot afford to look at life merely on how it affects or impacts me. But, we must consider our brother and sisters of all races, ethnicities and nationalities when contemplating our purpose.

What is my purpose? And, how will what I'm doing benefit me in the short term and in the long run? We are not thinking about how are vision impacts the lives of someone else, or if what we do is done indirectly. But, here we see how what we do or more importantly what we don't do could have a severe impact on someone else's life. We are not wired to think about others, but what we must realize is that our purpose was strategically created to help somebody else. We cannot afford to lose anyone, much in the same way we cannot afford to be distracted or to waste time, because ultimately someone's life is as stake. Someone's life hangs in the balance as we contemplate whether we are going to move forward with our purpose or are we going to live a life of distractions?

Why We Can't Afford to Be Distracted

You cannot afford to allow yourself to get distracted. Your life is far too important. You are far too valuable to waste your time living a distracted life. Wasting time is dangerous by-product of being distracted. Time is a diminishing commodity, because you never seem to have enough of it and once it's gone it cannot be replaced although everyone is given the same amount of time each day. What matters is how you make use of the time you have been given each day. God created us to be productive. His first commandment to Adam was to "be fruitful and multiply." Distraction is an enemy of productivity. You cannot be productive when you are distracted. You cannot be fruitful and multiply if you are distracted. You cannot fulfill God's first commandment to mankind if you are living a distracted life. If you are more concerned about what the other person is doing over what you are supposed to be doing, you are living a distracted life. And, the longer you live a distracted life, the more time that will be wasted, the more opportunities that will pass you by, the more dreams that will go unfulfilled, the less purposeful your life will become. You cannot afford to live distracted, because you end of up living your life through the lens of someone else's life and that's not how God intended for us to live. Our purpose was uniquely crafted and painstakingly designed for you and I, and it is not a one size fits all purpose, but your purpose was uniquely designed for you to fulfill. No one else can do what God created you to do. Out of the billions of people that walk this earth, there is no one else like you. Out of the billions of people that populate this earth, there is no one person that has the same fingerprint as you, there is no one with same DNA as you. This is a direct indication of the value that God has placed on your life. If there is no one on planet earth that has the same fingerprint as you, then that must mean that your life is not coincidental or haphazard, but your life is meaningful and intentional. Someone intended for us to be here; someone made sure that we were the only ones that could do what needed to be done. Our infinite value can be seen in the magnificence of our creation. The Bible tells us that we were "fearfully and wonderfully made." God is essentially saying to all of us, "Your life is so important that you're the only one that I gave it to." That's how much He thinks of us, to never have a duplicate of who He created. Our significance reflects the mind of God; He is so intentional and so methodical that everyone that lived and died had purpose. There was no one that entered this world that was not accompanied by purpose. It speaks volumes not just about the depths of the mind of God, but the enormity of His love for us. For His will to not contain duplicity; which simply means that what God has for me is essentially for me; that no one can have what God uniquely crafted for me, no one can be what God has called me to be. These are all reasons why we cannot afford to live a distracted life.

Dreams Deferred

Langston Hughes wrote about the consequences of distractions in his poem "Dreams Deferred." In it he gives explicit details on what happens to dreams that are literally wasted, he compares them to "spoiled or rotten meat." An otherwise filling and delectable protein is wasted, because it was left out and not properly stored in a refrigerated area. A benefit to no one not even the owner themselves. Likewise, dreams that have been wasted are usually those that have been discarded or abandoned by the dreamer, carelessly neglecting not just the tenets of the dream but the many people that could have benefited from the fruits thereof. Langston paints a very dark and bleak picture to depict the enormous impact of dreams that go unfulfilled. Imagine what our world we look like today if those who've contributed to its progress, the Rockefeller's, The Kennedy's, the Einstein's, the King's, the Tubman's, the Hamer's, The Carver's and many others whose dreams and visions we have benefited from and are still benefitting from, would have given up or succumb to the distractions that were designed to prevent them from accomplishing their goal. What kind of world would we live in? What would communication look like today had it not been for Alexander Graham Bell? Would we have electricity today had it not been for Benjamin Franklin on a windy, stormy night standing under a tree with a kite? What would the world of sports look like if not for the courage of Jackie Robinson to break baseball's color barrier and become the 1st African American to play Major League Baseball? What would the justice system of this country look like today if not for the likes of Thurgood Marshall, arguing for the rights of the disadvantaged people of this country? What would transportation look like today if it weren't for Henry Ford stepping out and creating the Model T; the world's first mass produced automobile? These were all dreamers, visionaries who were not satisfied looking at the world the way it was, but instead saw the world the way it could be. A quote from American novelist and philosopher; Ayn Rand, that really solidifies this notion of determination and perseverance in the face of sheer criticism and opposition regarding the emergence of a new invention or innovation. He said, solidifies this notion of determination and perseverance in the

"Throughout the centuries there were men who took first steps down new roads armed with nothing but their own vision. Their goals differed, but they all had this in common: that the step was first, the road new, the vision un-borrowed, and the response they received — hatred. The great creators — the thinkers, the artists, the scientists, the inventors — stood alone against the men of their time. Every great new thought was opposed. Every great new invention was denounced. The first motor was considered foolish. The airplane was considered impossible. The power loom was considered vicious. Anesthesia was considered sinful. But the men of unborrowed vision went ahead. They fought, they suffered and they paid. But they won."

The greatest travesty a dreamer could ever face is for their dreams to never become a reality. You must pursue your dreams, your goals, and your vision with every fiber of your being. You cannot let anything or anybody stop you from pursuing your dreams. Think of the countless people that could have benefited from your vision; think of the millions of lives that could have been saved if only you wouldn't have given up. Contextualizing vision this way puts it in its proper perspective, it places it on the plateau it belongs, because when a person sets out to fulfill a vision or a dream they are embarking upon a grand endeavor whose impact may be felt for generations and generations to come. And one thing you must understand is that the size of the endeavor often time determines the size of the obstacle that is headed your way. Great visions and dreams are always met with great obstacles and hurdles to overcome. The greatness of the vision is not meted out primarily because of its size, but it's opposition. You can't endeavor to be great without expecting some great opposition, without some great criticism, without even some great defeats. Your opposition is the proving ground for your greatness. How you handle pressure, how you handle opposition, how you handle your enemy will ultimately determine what kind of leader you will become. Conversely, if you don't have any opposition, if you don't have anything or anybody challenging you, then you are not doing very much. If you do not have any obstacles in your path, if you don't have anything or anyone trying their hardest to stop you, then your vision isn't that big. We have always been taught to run away from trouble or that trouble carries with it no socially redeeming value. Not so! But, often times you discover who you really are by the enemy that's chasing you. "I must be valuable to somebody," "I must really be somebody, if every time I look up here they come." The spiritual rule of thumb is the adversary wouldn't be chasing you if you weren't doing something. You have to be going somewhere if you are enemy is constantly chasing you. Ask yourself, what am I doing that's attracting so much negative attention? Why do they want to stop me? What would have happened if they did? These are critical questions that every visionary leader must grapple with whenever you endeavor to dream.

Biggest Takeaway

One of the most important takeaways of this book is that life is not arbitrary but it is purposeful and meaningful. It is such because our creation is a result of someone else's creative thinking about what our lives would be. When we look at our lives from this perspective, we can start to see the purpose and meaning intertwined throughout our life. Purpose and meaning are not only endowed unto mankind, but it is also endued upon the entire universe that we marvel and contemplate as the greatest enterprise of human existence. It's hard not to see purpose and meaning manifested in every nook and cranny of our universe. And, with that in mind have you ever wondered if you were fulfilling your purpose? Have you ever wondered if you were on the path that God originally intended for you in the beginning? When you examine the correlation between time and purpose you must understand that God's timing far exceeds mankind's realm of comprehension. We can forget trying to understand or to even comprehend the timing of God. This is a critical piece, because we believe time is linear and it continues in forward progression at a relentless pace that never stops, pauses or rewinds for any conceivable circumstance or reason. Even though, we; at times, want to hit the pause button or rewind button and do somethings over or slow things down a bit. But, we cannot stop, pause or rewind time, we just have to catch up to its rhythmic pace in order to discover the revelation of our true purpose. Our purpose is revealed through time. Like an onion, our Creator chooses to reveal to us our purpose in layers or baby steps, because He knows if it was given to us all at once we would not be able to handle it. The luxury of time affords us the privilege as well as the opportunity to look back at some of history's more influential figures and apply this simply principle. Imagine if Barack Obama was told upon his birth that he would become the first Black President of the United States; he would ascend to this highest office in the world and become our nation's 44th President. What do you think his response would have been? If Michael Jordan was told when he was first cut from his high school basketball team, "not to worry", "don't give up", because in a few years you are going to become the most recognizable athlete in sports history. What do you think he would have said? What if Neil Armstrong was told as a young man in high school that he would be the first man to walk on the surface of the moon, what do you think his response would've been? We understand that these individual's accomplishments were not coincidental moments in time, but they were strategically thought out and well-planned events that made up the circumference of each their individual lives. And, time was the medium that was used to mete out the discovery of their purpose, because time is as important to the discovery of purpose as purpose itself. We cannot discount time or even speed up time to accommodate our selfish needs and desires, but we must seek the will of the Creator to receive the precious gift of purpose. Everyone has a purpose; there wasn't a single person born into this universe that was not created without it. For some of us we want to be operating in our purpose at a certain age, where we can easily see how functioning within this capacity will impact the rest of our lives. And, in some cases God does reveal it to us earlier in life where we can see how time and purpose go hand in hand in mapping out our destiny. In other cases, it is not as cut and dry. The great thing about God is that He is not a cookie-cutter Creator. He doesn't do the same thing for everybody; He doesn't even do the same thing twice.

Adam and Eve

Distractions are what caused Adam and Even to forfeit their divine inheritance in the Garden of Eden; focusing more of their attention on the tree that they couldn't eat over the abundance of fruit and vegetation from the plethora of other trees they could eat without reproach. And, when you examine and study the dynamics of what actually took place in the Garden, you will discover the enormous consequences of distractions and the tremendous pain they cause. God tells Adam while walking him through the vast Garden that He just created, that you can eat of anything in this Garden. You have access to everything in the north, south, east and west corners of this Garden. All the fruits, and vegetation, the entire geography of this Garden is yours to keep watch over. And, that in and of itself should have been enough to satisfy Adam's appetite for dominion and power. God created everything in the Garden, and put Adam in charge of it. Adam didn't have to carry the burden of creation, the only responsibility he had was to oversee the Garden that God had created. We must believe that Adam was a very intelligent human being. The Bible speaks of Adams immense intelligence, when it reveals his ability to name every creature that God created, and the names that Adam gave them are the same names that they have today. The memory that Adam was given by God to retain the names of every animal that was created; this was a clear illustration of the dominion that man had been given by God in the closing verses of the 2nd Chapter in Genesis. God not only created man, but He equipped man to do what God expected for him to do. That being, said the gravity of the power and the dominion that Adam had was reflective in the vast real-estate of the Garden that God sought fit to put him over. There was no greater indication of the trust that God had in who He created, by divesting His power of authority into this one man. Adam had absolutely nothing to do with the creation of the Garden, and yet God put him over it as the caretaker of it. What a tremendous privilege that Adam was afforded by God to be the one to watch over the Garden that God-Himself, created. To have unlimited access to everything in the Garden, to know that everything in the Garden is subject to your authority and dominion, that only God-the Creator of the world, is the only one greater than you, this is just a snapshot of Adam's preeminence in the Garden. And, when you juxtapose Adam's authority and dominion to what ultimately became his downfall, you begin to see the gravity of this word distraction, especially when you consider all that Adam loss for the taste of what was forbidden.

Adam lost everything in a matter of seconds for something that he thought would give him more than he already had. Adam ate of the fruit of the Tree of Good and Evil, which is a tree that God told him and Eve not to eat from or they would surely die. And instead of enjoying everything that God had given him access to in the Garden, Adam became preoccupied with that which was forbidden. Isn't that just like us; to focus all our attention on that which we can't have over that which we already have? What is it about someone else's possessions that are more attractive than what we have? And, the danger of distraction is that you end up undervaluing what you have to the point of losing what you have, only to discover that it was more valuable than you thought it was. Unfortunately, it is not until it is gone that we are then able to clearly see how valuable it really was. What a tragedy! This is the dilemma that has befallen every human being since Adam. We always seem to appreciate what someone else has over what we already have, and we only end up devaluing what we have to the point of losing it only to discover it was more valuable than we thought it was. Such was the case with Adam, who only after disobeying God and eating of the forbidden fruit realized the gravity of what he had done. Once he and his wife Eve were removed from the Garden and they had to find food and shelter for themselves on their own, did they realize the immense value of what they had before. The power of distractions. It can cause you to lose your focus, your drive, your motivation. It can cause you to overlook your own value and self-worth, because of what you see in something or someone else.

Why do we always seem to be more focused on the things that we don't have more than that which we do have? Why does the grass always seem greener on the other side? How can what we don't have to take up so much space in our mental closet? It appears to be a natural propensity for mankind to live their lives looking over their shoulder wondering what the next man has that they don't have. The answers to these questions are a harsh reality into the lives of many people who live their lives vicariously through other people, primarily because they are unhappy with the life they have been given. Depressed about what you don't have vs being appreciative and grateful for that which you do have, this is what this chronic behavior typically produces. What an empty existence constantly dwelling on things they don't have, can't afford, haven't done, and to allow that to completely occupy your thinking. The result is you end up doing nothing but continuing to ruminate and worry about things that you can't change. Distractions is what this behavior amounts to, because it causes us to focus the lion share of our attention on frivolous and fruitless thinking. Thinking that doesn't produce any positive results, in fact it's thinking that doesn't produce any results.

The Dangers of Distractions

One of the dangerous effects of distraction is wasted time. Distractions that result in wasted time is the greatest and most egregious consequence of being distracted. What it does is causes you to take your focus off your purpose, and whenever your trajectory is taken off of your purpose you become your own worst enemy. You are ultimately standing in the way of your own success; your own blessing. You cannot afford to live a life filled with distractions, and yet this is the greatest weapon, and the greatest tragedy that has befallen God's creation. We have become distracted; distracted by the cares of this world; distracted by our own foolish self-interests, distracted by the supernatural devices of the enemy. These have had a lasting effect on the lives of all of mankind. At one time or another we all have been effected by the distractions of each of these worldly and supernatural tactics, to cause us to divert our attention off our God-given purpose. But, why would the enemy want to stop you? Why would you be a primary target on the enemy's radar to stop? If you ever want to really find out who you are, ask your haters; ask those who are secretly working against you. Ask the ones who are plotting your demise; ask the ones who are diametrically opposed to everything you stand for. In a very real way, you've made an impact even in their lives, which has caused them to commit themselves to working against you. There is no greater example of this than the devil-himself. The devil has committed his entire existence to the total destruction and annihilation of the Child of God. The Bible says in St. John 10:10, (KJV) "the thief cometh not but for to steal, kill and destroy". And, when you examine the nature of these three words, you begin to discover the diabolical plan of the devil. The devil not only wants to steal; or take everything that he can from you, but he also wants to physically kill you, and not only does he want to physically kill; as if that wasn't enough already, but he wants to destroy your soul as well. The devil wants to destroy any chance you may have of being what God created you to be. He wants to erase your very existence. Therein lies the essence of the devil's angst against us. What God created you to be is the true essence of your purpose, what God created you to be is the fulfillment of what He saw for you before the foundations of the world. So, if the devil can destroy that chance, he will essentially be spitting in the face of God. It would be the devil's ultimate revenge against God. Each person that he manipulates into thinking less of themselves is one strike for him in the win column. But, just think of how significant your life is even to him, if he has dedicated his entire existence to wiping you out. You must be somebody, if you are on the devil's radar, you must be somebody if you are keeping the devil busy coming up with ways to stop you, you must be somebody if you are the devil's motivation to stay on his job of destroying you.

It might sound a bit strange to see ourselves through the eyes of our enemy, but it is an interesting perspective to consider. All of us have enemies, all of us have somebody that is committed to seeing us fall, all us of have somebody in our life that is dedicated to seeing your demise. Why, because you matter to somebody, your life is filled with purpose; even when you cannot see it, even when it may not be clear to you. It's amazing how others can see your light even when you have a hard time seeing it yourself. The enemy can see the light in you, they can see the potential the rest within you and it is their primary motivation every day to stop you.

Others can see your light, even when you think you have well-hidden it behind a bushel. Who you are is the reason you have so many haters; who you are is the reason you are faced with so much adversity. What God has gifted you to do is the reason you can't sleep at night. And, as soon as you realize this the better off you will be.

The Impact of Your Purpose

What is also amazing to consider in all of this is the impact of your purpose, and how that effects the people in your circle as well as those who are outside of your circle. The reality is there are positive as well negative impacts to your purpose. Everyone is not happy about your success; everyone is not going to be happy to see you win; everyone is not going to celebrate your victories, and the sooner you realize this the better off you'll be. You cannot allow the motives and perceptions of other people to become a distraction to you. You're too busy trying to figure out what other folk are up to that you have lost track of where you are supposed to be on this journey we call life. Or, you are caught in what other people's perception of you might be. This is another common distraction for a lot of people. They are so worried about what people think of them that they are content playing it safe and avoiding any potential risks for fear of public opinion. But, you can't be afraid of what people are going to think; you can't be fearful of what folk are going to say about you stepping outside of your comfort zone to achieve something better; something greater. You cannot let other people's perceptions deter you from pursuing your dreams and visions. It is easy for us to consider the positive impact of our purpose, and how the fulfillment of our God-given purpose will positively affect those who God has ordained for us to touch. But, at the same time just as much as our purpose is blessing to some people, it is also cursing others as well. It makes the devil sick to his stomach to see God's people prosper; it gives the devil a coronary arrest to see God's people overcome the obstacles that he's set in their way to destroy them. He gets mad when God's people are glad. It upsets his equilibrium when God's people can rise above their adversity. And, why wouldn't it; after all he's dedicated his entire existence to our downfall, so when the opposite happens then you should expect him to be angry and upset.

If nothing else when you begin to spiritually analyze the weapon of distraction, you can begin to see why it is such an important weapon in the devil's arsenal. Consequently, if he can distract you away from your purpose, you have voluntarily or involuntary joined his. When you are distracted by the devil, you become an accessory to your own demise. And, yes, the devil wins again, because now you have become a willing partner with him in the destruction of yourself. This is the apex of his existence; to get God's precious creation to turn on themselves and destroy each other. This is how badly the devil wants us all destroyed. And, again what better way to do that than to corrupt the "Apple of God's Eye." What would God think of His precious creation now that they have been corrupted by their primary adversary-the devil?

The Dash

One writer said, "Time waits for no man," which essentially means that the hour glass of time doesn't stop for anyone. But, its eternal hand continues to turn whether we are actively doing something, or even standing still. The concept of distraction intersects with the ever-present reality of time and there you have the essence of the phrase "a waste of time." When time is wasted, you are essentially being distracted from your purpose or a goal that you could be constructively working toward. Distractions are the enemy of time, because the commodity of time is now wasted when it is not used doing something productive. I once heard it said of someone's life that, "he died empty." On the surface that sounds somewhat troubling, because it appears that what is being said is that they died penniless or they died broke, implicitly suggesting that they're life at death had no value. But, quite to the contrary, the message that is being conveyed is of a much deeper and weightier elk than what is seen on the surface. What is actually being said of this person's life is that they died not taking with them unfulfilled promises or dreams, but they accomplished everything they set out to do. He died with nothing left to give, because he lived a full and accomplished life. Dying leaving a lasting legacy is the same as saying he died empty. He took nothing with him, because he left everything of value behind for the world to benefit from. He died empty is the same as saying he died fulfilled, because there was nothing left for him or her to do but to close their eyes knowing that what they were created to do they did and they did it to the best of their ability.

Conversely, there are those who died never accomplishing their dreams or visions. They died full of vision, full of untapped potential. This is why the graveyard is said to be one of the richest places in the world. No, it's not Fort Knox, it's not the Pyramid's in Egypt or the treasure hidden in Dubai or some other distant place, but it is the graveyard. This is so, because this is the one place that contains the world's reservoir of untapped potential; million-dollar ideas that were never pursued; dreams that Langston referred to as "rotten and spoiled meat" that have long since expired with the fated remains of the dreamer. What a sad state of affairs. So, in the final analysis, what really matters is what you do with the time you have; what really matters is what you do with "the dash" that is pointedly placed right between the day you were "born" and the day you "die." Although, some would argue that those are not the two most important dates of our life anyhow. The two most important dates in your life are the day you were born and they day you figure out why.

Imagine if everyone that God created was walking in and living out their purpose, what a wonderful world this would be. Unfortunately, for so many people they don't know their purpose, because they don't know the Originator of their purpose. And, there is no way you could ever know who you are if you don't know who God is. Likewise, you'll never discover your purpose until you are formally introduced to the Author of your purpose. Getting to know Him, you in turn will discover who you are. I believe it was Socrates who said, " …an unexamined life is a life not worth living," he was right on one front that without a proper examination of one's life at some point, you'll never know its true value. But, what Socrates neglects to mention is that your examination of life is not a solo venture, however it must be with the Giver of Life who will in turn show you the value in living.

The Chase

Distractions are the one of the No.1 weapons the enemy uses to keep us from being what God wants us to be. If the devil can keep you distracted, you'll never be what God predestined for you to be. You will continue to be pre-occupied with whatever machinations the devil brings to keep you off focus. Simply put, distractions are a direct indication that there is something that the devil doesn't want you to see. There is something that the devil is trying to keep you from visualizing, and what is that? The devil wants so badly to keep you blind to the truth of who you really are. If you only knew who you were, you would be dangerous in the kingdom. If you knew who you were there would be no way the devil could get you to settle for anything less. It is only those unfamiliar with their true worth that continuously settle for things that are utterly beneath them. The devil's objective is to keep you distracted so that you don't ever realize the potential you have within you to become the giant God created you to be. What's interesting is the lengths that the devil will go to keep you distracted. In fact, your life outside of Christ is nothing but an elaborate distraction orchestrated by the devil himself. The trinkets and bobbles that the devil parades in front of you are symbols of wealth and extravagance that he entices you to chase, because those are symbols of wealth and extravagance that are made to appear to be symbols of self-worth. And, so he's got you chasing money and chasing things, instead of seeking God for the life He designed for you to lead. The irony behind the chase is that your value far exceeds anything the devil parades in front of you, but because of this game of distraction he has successfully played with your mind, you engage in this seemingly endless, mindless activity of self-worth never able to understand why am I going around in circles? I heard someone once give the illustration about expensive automobiles that makes the explicit correlation between how God sees us and how we should see ourselves. They said, Bentley and Rolls Royce never have to advertise, because their value is understood. Their value doesn't need to be clarified; in other words, their value literally speaks for itself. Subsequently, our value and worth need not be advertised, inasmuch as our value and worth should speak for itself. The painstaking and meticulous care that our Creator invested into His creation speaks volumes about His expectations for us. He didn't create us to have to further validate our worth, but by virtue of the reputation of the Creator we are direct recipients of His immense value by association.

The reality is the enemy should always be chasing you, which means that you are going in a direction that they are attempting to prevent you from going. However, when the enemy has you chasing things instead of chasing your destiny, he can stop running because when you're chasing things it is a road that leads to nowhere, which is exactly the direction he wants you to go. Checkmate! Someone once said that if you if you don't have any haters then you are not doing very much, and Bishop TD Jakes added to that by saying, "I've never had a hater doing better than me." Your paradigm of success should always have the enemy chasing you, because you are essentially leading them and they're behind you. However, when you engage the enemy on any level you have essentially stop leading and you are now chasing them down a road that leads to nowhere. The only thing worth chasing is your purpose.

Stay Focused

Staying focus is one of the key ways to defeat the distractions that life may bring to obstruct your vision and keep you from achieving your goals. Staying focus sounds like a pretty simple solution, but it was one that is highly effective if implemented properly. To stay focus is the optimal objective and in many cases, is easier said than done, because life's distractions sometimes come with much more enticements and attractions that causes us to lose our focus and get distracted. But, staying focus is key to realizing the vision that God has placed inside each and every one of us. If staying focus was easy then this section would be completely unnecessary, but we all need a reminder every now and then to stay on task and keep moving towards achieving our goals. I'm sure this is the kind of advice that every successful person has heard at one time or another. Staying focus must certainly be a part of the regiment of success that every participant has partaken of in order to enjoy the fruits of their labor. I'm positive this advice has made it into the locker rooms of athletes all over the world in every sport. Especially when the goal is to be the best at whatever sport you pursue.

A young boy has dreams of becoming a basketball player, so his father puts up a hoop in the backyard and everyday he spends an hour outside working on his game. Dribbling, running layup lines, shooting free throws, all with the expectation of getting better. Each day the young boy comes home from school, eats dinner, finishes his homework just in time to end the day with an hour's worth of practice out on the basketball court. All while he is shooting, he's visualizing himself playing in college or professionally for his favorite NBA team against his favorite player. And, this image is what keeps this young boy motivated each day to come home and practice this game he loves so much. It's because he's sees himself doing better than what he is right now. He's sees a future that hasn't yet materialized, but it is very much a possibility if he is willing to do what it takes to get there. Something comes up that interrupts his daily regiment; friends stop by to take him away from the game he loves and so he doesn't get to spend time working on his craft. He tries out for the team at school and he doesn't make it, so disappointment sets in and doesn't practice as much or as often. Things start to pop up to pull this young boy's focus away from realizing his dream, and the longer you are distracted the less likely you are to return to where you started.

I admire people that overcome insurmountable odds to achieve great success. It takes a great deal of focus and stamina to keep doing something that no one said you would be able to do. Michael Jordan was cut from his high school basketball team as a youngster starting out playing the game he would eventually learn to dominate. You wouldn't think that this was a part of his story, because we are so used to seeing him dominate the game of basketball night in and night out as a superstar athlete for the Chicago Bulls. But, his greatness didn't begin with winning championships and cutting down nets, but his greatness came by way of defeat. He could have easily decided at that point early in life that his high school basketball coach was right to cut him; his coach could probably see that basketball was not the sport for Michael at the time. Michael; like that young boy, could have easily given up, quit and went in a completely different direction. However, as history would have it that was not the decision that Mr. Jordan decided to make. In fact, he did the exact opposite of quitting, he got more engaged, more determined, and more focused to never allow this to ever happened again. I'm told that Michael Jordan has a competitive nature that won't allow him to get distracted, his success is a by-product of his unrelenting focus. He is constantly challenging himself, pushing himself to be better than he was the day before. And this is how we have to be when it comes to realizing the vision that we have in our minds. Quitting is easy; it doesn't take much effort to quit or to give up, doesn't take much thought to throw in the towel. But, why is it so much harder to stay the course, to stay focus, to continue, to endure, to preserve. The reason it is so much harder is because the reward is so much greater in the end.

Embedded within this concept of staying focus is the understanding that you don't have time to waste, and that time is a fleeting mechanism that continues to turn even when we are standing still. We continue to age even when we are doing nothing, and this is a reality of life. And, because time is fleeting, we can ill-afford to allow even one minute of our time to be wasted being distracted from pursuing our life's purpose. Staying focus also means that you are constantly readjusting and recalibrating your lens to see your vision better and more clearly. Distractions come to blur our vision and to cause us to lose focus, and we end of drifting in the opposite direction of where our purpose is trying to take us. The enemy sends distractions our way, because he knows the value of the purpose God has placed inside of you. And, if he can keep you distracted you will not only never fulfill your purpose, but those you were assigned to impact because of your purpose will be left hanging in the balance because you decided to allow your distractions to preoccupy your mind.

Chapter 6

CLEAR VISION

"The only thing worse than being blind is having sight but no vision.
— Hellen Keller

Anyone who knows me knows that I am a big Michigan State Football and Basketball fan. In addition to being a proud alumnus of this great institution, there is no greater fan of these two sports than yours truly. I have been a fan of MSU for as long as I can remember. I have enjoyed the good times and endured the bad ones, and here recently we have been experiencing a long-awaited renaissance in both sports that is extremely gratifying. MSU has two great storied programs in basketball and football, producing such greats as Magic Johnson, Greg Kelser, Kirk Gibson, Bubba Smith, Andre Rison, Derrick Mason, Le'Veon Bell, Kirk Cousins and Draymond Green just to name a few. And, this program has with it some impressive Hall of Fame Coaches that have guided it to where it is today; Duffy Daugherty, George Perles, Nick Saban, Mark Dantonio, Judd Heathcote and Tom Izzo. All great coaches who left an indelible mark on this great land-grant institution. Recently, the football program under Mark Dantonio has experienced some remarkable accomplishments which; I believe, are a direct reflection of its determined leader, Mark Dantiono. Coach Dantonio is a rock solid, determined and polished leader of this program, who prides himself on instilling into his players discipline and determination. Before becoming head coach at MSU, Coach Dantonio served as an Assistant Coach under Nick Saban at MSU, and then served as Defensive Coordinator under Jim Tressel at Ohio State winning a National Championship and going on to become the Head Coach for the Cincinnati Bear Cats. Dantonio became the Head Coach at MSU back in 2004 and has taken this program to heights it hasn't seen in quite some time. One memorable moment in program history not just for me but for the entire Spartan nation was our trip to the Rose Bowl to play Stanford back in 2013. This game was the culmination of a spectacular year that begin with a trip that Dantonio took to Pasadena-himself to do some recruiting. But, while he was there he had an opportunity to tour the great coliseum known as the "Rose Bowl" and he took a video that he would share with his players about his vision for the program for the upcoming year. This video that he took at the Rose Bowl was to be the team's motivation not just for the year, but a prophetic message of destiny that would ultimately lead this team back to these hallowed grounds to play in what was one of the biggest games in this program's history. And what was most significant about this moment was that Dantonio's visit to the Rose Bowl was as much for him as it was for his team, because how can you visualize a place that you've never been. It so much better when you have been where you trying to tell someone else they have the potential to go. Your words seem to mean more, when they are tempered with experience, especially when you are in a position of leadership. When you are trying to get a group of people to buy into your leadership, where you've been and what you've experienced is just as important as your ability to lead. Getting his players to believe in his message as the coach of the team was extremely important, because if you are a leader that can't get anyone to follow you, you are; as my sainted father in the gospel Bishop David Ellis use to say, "just another man out for a walk." Coach Dantonio was not that kind of a leader, but he possessed a gift to motivate his young players, and this gift to motivate was reflected on as well as off the field.

So, for Dantonio this trip to Pasadena was a pilgrimage of sorts that he took by himself, but one that he eventually shared with his team so that they could visualize a place they had never been, but to get there they would have to go to a level that had only imagined. I saw the video during the pre-game of the Rose Bowl, as the commentator talked about Dantonio's momentous trip to Pasadena months before his team would ever set foot within the hallowed walls of this great sports cathedral. And, I began to think about the significance of this video and what it might have meant to his team back home to see their coach talking to them from the Rose Bowl, telling them that this is the place where we will be next January. This is the place that the fruits of our season will send us, if we stay focus, stay vigilante, stay determined, and stay committed to our goal of winning. And, I watched as the team embraced the theme for the year, "Chase It," and just as the theme suggests they chased the goal of making it to the 100th Rose Bowl every play of every game that year only losing to Notre Dame. MSU would go 11-1 and make it to the very destination their coach prophetically spoke of an entire year earlier. And not only would the Spartans have the privileged to play in this historic game, but the same momentum that it took to get them their they would strategically use as motivation to win this game and forever be cemented in history as the team that won the 100th Rose Bowl.

You Got to See It Before You See It

Visualization is the tool that Coach Dantonio used to motivate his players to believe they could play in a game they had never played in before. Through the powerful medium of video, the coach was able to take his players to a place they had never been before. In essence, what Coach Dantonio realized is that the idea had to be birthed somewhere. And, that for his players to believe, they needed to see it before they see it. Studies have shown that people are very visual and if they can view a video associated with a story or a cause it is far more impactful than if they saw a flier or read an article about the subject matter. Video has been and is still being used as a motivational tool in locker rooms and even board rooms around the world. It has also been used in other ways as well. We've seen the impact that video has had on the recent police shootings of unarmed black men, and how these events carry with them more significance because the world can see these shootings and make their own conclusions and judgements of what happened. These same events if there were no video evidence associated with these shootings they probably wouldn't have gotten as much national attention as they eventually did. Subsequently, we can see the impact of having video footage verses an eye witness account of what happened. Video seems to carry more weight. But, I digress. However, this is only one type of visualization, there is also such a concept as conscious or subconscious visualization, which simply means that the images one sees are purely mentally driven. This is yet another example of how powerful the mind is that we can visualize a reality that hasn't materialized yet, and believe in it so strongly and profusely that we will work towards achieving it merely on the notion of experiencing the tangible result of what we've seen. For example, a freshman in college visualizes the day they will walk across the stage and graduate, and every day of their matriculation in college this is not only the image they see but also the motivation they have to achieve this goal. I know it sounds simpler than it actually is, but there is great virtue in self-motivation, being able to see yourself in a new light that you haven't seen before, and this was all initiated within your own mind.

What Coach Dantonio did in this video was to incorporate a methodology called "vV that essentially capsulizes a single moment into a motivational tool to inspire an even bigger and greater opportunity. Through the lens of modern technology, Coach Dantonio spoke to his players from a pre-recorded message taken hundreds of thousands of miles away at a place that his players could not physically go, but through this medium they could see themselves not just through the lens of the camera but through the inspiring words of their coach. Visualization became the motivational tool that was used to inspire that team to reach heights that many didn't believe were possible. What was understood in that moment was that it is important to visually see where you want to go. Coach Dantonio could have spoken to his team about his trip after he returned home and gave the same speech he did on the video from the field at the Coliseum. He could have given it with this same fervor and the same excitement he had in the video, and it probably would have motivated his team as well. But, actually being on the field and speaking to his team from those hallowed grounds, allowed his message to resonate even further because it came from the same place he believed the Spartans could ultimately go. He gave his team the unique opportunity to not just see it in their "mind's eye" but to physically see what many may have never seen before. And, I know you're probably thinking to yourself, he is probably overshooting the impact of a simple recruiting trip. If this is your first inclination after reading this account, you've either underestimated the impact of such an experience or you're a University of Michigan fan. In either case, I will forgive your ignorance and encourage you to see this as more than just a recruiting video, but a life's lesson that can help you in your own personal endeavors.

It is extremely important as you pursue your own goals and dreams that you visualize them already being accomplished. You must see yourself going where you've never been, accomplishing what you never thought possible, or achieving that insurmountable goal. You have to essentially "see it" before you "see it." In essence, you first must believe it's possible before it will ever be possible. And, you don't necessarily have to physically see it; while using video is highly effective in this case, it is not the only way one can visualize themselves doing something without actually having done it. This is why the mind is such a powerful weapon if used properly. It can be an extremely helpful mechanism when it comes to utilizing this tool powerful tool of visualization. Every successful person has used the powerful tool of visualization at one time or another. Every dream, vision or idea had to begin somewhere, and in most cases, they all were birthed in the mind. The mind is the birthplace of our dreams and visions. The mind is our mental playground where our dreams and aspirations can run free of criticism, free of doubt, free of limitations or boundaries. Our mind can become the breeding ground for endless possibilities, if we allow it to cultivate our imagination instead of stifling it. What a powerful tool that God has given us when used properly.

The Concept of Visualization

The concept of visualization is a powerful tool for goal setting. You have to be able to visualize a future reality that hasn't yet materialized if you're ever going to experience what you've only seen. Many successful people from all walks of life have used this tool of visualization to see what cannot be seen. Visualization is a motivational tool that successful people use to influence them to keep moving in spite of a reality that is riddled with obstacles and setbacks that may suggest that what you have you seen in your mind's eye will never materialize. Athletes, businessmen, actors and actresses, musicians and the like all use this powerful tool to see a future they have yet to experience. Synonymous with visualization is perception, because how you see things ultimately will determine what you will see.

How do you engage in visualization? Some choose to get away from distractions and separate themselves from people; any negative influences they will discourage them from desiring to see a different reality. Physically separating yourself from people nowadays is not enough, today with the advent of social media you have to get off of social media which can be another un-welcomed distraction. It's amazing how powerful social media has become, and the proliferation of social media platforms have increased at a staggering rate. From Facebook and Twitter, to Instagram and Snap Chat, hundreds more are cropping up, which carries with them their own set of advantages and disadvantages. So, when it comes time to get away mentally, it's not just a physical separation, you have to turn off cellphones and smart devices, PCs and tablets that connect you to your various social media accounts that can also work against your desire to cancel out all of the background noise of life so that you can foster the kind of mental environment that is needed in order to properly engage in the process of visualization.

"You got to see it before you see it," speaks to the power of visualization. Visualization is one of the keys to realizing your vision, you have got to mentally, psychologically and most importantly spiritually see the success that you are determined to achieve. You have got to mentally see it before you will physically see it. Being able to visualize your success will help get closer to actually achieving it. Visualization is a form of internal motivation that one needs in order to stay focused on realizing your goals

Exposure

An important component of visualization is exposure, one thing takes place in the mind, while the latter component lends itself to more of a physical nature. The two; however, go hand-in-hand. Exposure is a key component of visualization, because if you can be physically exposed to the environment you were once only able to see either in your "mind's eye" or through some other medium of technology this will bring you one step closer to doing what you once thought you could only see. There is unlimited value and virtue that accompanies exposure, because sometimes it is good to see yourself naturally where you never thought you'd be. This becomes the incentive you need to continue pursuing a vision or a dream that once only resided in the subtle recesses of your mind's eye. And, now that you are physically where you saw yourself mentally, you can now begin to put the puzzle pieces together of how I can accomplish the vision that will put me here not as a one-time visitor, but as an accomplished resident of this new reality. For some people, all they need is to be physically exposed to where they want to be, and this is all the incentive they need to keep working towards becoming an actual resident of this reality. What exposure does is gives the impetuous person an ability to see themselves in a new light, with new possibility and with new potential. The potential and possibility has always been there, but you had to be exposed to a new environment to see what was lying dormant within you. Your present reality has to be stretched in order for you to see the potential that rests within you. In other words, you can't see your real potential until your reality has been challenged. I believe this is what is missing in the lives of so many people, the reason they are not better is because they have never been challenged to be better, or do better. Essentially, the potential rests within all of us, but it is not until that potential is unearthed or discovered, it will never be realized. And, exposure is the mechanism that causes your potential to be discovered. A better characterization of this concept is when pressure or friction has been applied to a briquette of coal. The coal doesn't know its own transformative power until friction has been applied to its surface and this immense pressure is applied to this otherwise dormant piece of energy. However, once applied this briquette of coal is transformed into a priceless diamond whose value far exceeds the depths of what we thought possible. Exposure works for us much in the same way, because once we have been taken out of an environment where we were immensely comfortable; and taken on a guided tour of a space that could potentially become our reality, our internal senses are awakened and we begin to realize that this new reality is more attainable than we thought previously, and this exposure almost serves as a foretaste of the person we have yet to become. A practical example of this concept of exposure is an internship or mentorship, because what this experience does it takes you completely out of your comfort zone and places in a space where you want to be but never thought possible. This new experience is actually a mental shock to your system, because now you are on a guided tour of what could possibly become your new reality.

You Cannot See Without Vision

Hellen Keller was quoted as saying, "You cannot see without a vision." A very insightful declaration coming from a woman who was both blind and deaf from a child. On the surface, one would think she was speaking to her own deficiencies or handicaps in her natural inability to see and therefore because she couldn't see naturally, she naturally wouldn't have vision. From a practical standpoint, this would be a true statement. Someone that is physically blind and cannot see would not have the ability to have natural vision. But, this would also appear to be a realistic expectation of being naturally blind, why would this statement merit any special consideration? In a sense, she is saying something that every sighted and un-sighted person already knows, "you cannot see without a vision." But, is that really what Helen Keller is trying to say? Especially, coming from someone that history records as the first deaf and blind person to earn a Bachelor of Arts degree. This statement coming from someone with this kind of background was not speaking in natural terms. But, Helen Keller was speaking both symbolically, metaphorically and I believe even spiritually when it comes to the merits of having a vision. And, for a blind person to coin such a phrase or to have such insight into the significance of vision is extraordinary. I don't believe she was speaking negatively about her physical condition; by no means, but I believe she was illustrating the importance of being able to see what you can't see. There are some things in life that you are going to have to see in your "mind's eye" before they will ever materialize before your "natural eyes." Things that you are going to have to see mentally, and spiritually before they will ever manifest themselves in reality. This speaks to the magnitude of the process of visualization; being able to visualize what you desire to happen even before it happens, and for that vision to become the primary motivating force to realize what may seem to be impossible. In the case of Helen Keller, she saw her Bachelors of Arts Degree in her hand before she even signed up for her first class. This is the type of vision, she was referring to; to be so motivated and so inspired to achieve greatness that it becomes the vision that guides you from conception to reality. You can see the manifestation of your reality while you are still matriculating through the process, and this vision is what keeps you going, it's what keeps you up at night, it becomes your driving force to achieve greatness. It's the kind of vision even a blind person has, and Helen Keller profundity proved.

Another reason why this quote from Helen Keller is so telling is because, from a sighted person's perspective you would think that natural sight would have to be the preoccupation of the unsighted person, especially due to the fact that natural sight is something that they presently do not have. Not being able to physically see would have to be at the forefront of their mind, because the absence of natural sight would seem to be a consistent reality that they are reminded of each and every day they wake up. This would also probably apply to handicap or disable person(s) in general, because whatever physical ability you lack as a result of a physical deformity of some kind would have to be "front and center" of their thinking. That being said, the absence of natural sight to a blind person would be tantamount to a sighted person losing a limb, natural sight would seem to be paramount to their survival. But, for Helen Keller; who was blind and deaf from birth, to evoke such a powerful statement of vision and not be talking about the type of vision that she-herself lacks is remarkable. And, what is even more remarkable than that is she is essentially saying that you can be physically blind and still have vision or conversely, you can have physical sight and have no vision. What a remarkable analysis from an already remarkable figure in history. You don't need physical sight to have vision, but you need vision if you ever want to truly see. Having this kind of vision transcends natural sight. Her life exudes this remarkably, inasmuch as she not only believed what she said but she lived it as well. For her not to dwell on what she lacked, but to put emphasis and focus and what she did have; this is the true recipe for success. Some people tend to dwell on what they lack, and spend countless hours ruminating over what they don't have. However, it is a truly mentally and spiritually liberated person that doesn't waste time dwelling on what they don't have, but instead spend time visualizing and seeing new possibilities and opportunities even in the midst of a limited reality. Ms. Keller truly speaks from a position of power in this regard, because even though she was physically deaf and blind, she didn't allow those physical disabilities to disable her thinking. She did not allow what she could not do physically to limit her mentally or spiritually. Here is a person; from my estimation, that should have every reason to murmur and complain about their reality. If there ever was a person that should have probably been given a pass because of their physical disabilities it should have been Helen Keller, However, when you examine the essence of her truest beliefs, she would protest and proclaim, "Don't pity me, pity the one that can see but has no vision." This is the person that truly deserves your pity. They are the ones that are truly handicap, according to her analysis.

"You cannot see without vision" is the problem as well as the solution for a lot of people in our world today. So many people that have purpose, that have promise but lack a vision for themselves. It's true you can have purpose and you can have promise, which essentially equates to having the potential for success, but without a clear plan, without a vision there to guide you and motivate you, you are essentially spinning your wheels; going nowhere fast. Purpose and promise was given to all of us even before the worlds were formed, which means that no one is here by accident or happenstance, everyone is here on purpose, by purpose and for a purpose. The problem is we haven't sought out the Creator of All Things to find out what that purpose is for our lives. If you want to examine someone with vision, you must look with critical eyes at the Creator, because this great enterprise we call the world was created by His own spoken word. His vision for mankind became manifested in the first five words in the Bible, "In the beginning God created …" I know we've spent a lot of time already discussing this massive enterprise called Earth, and it's surrounding neighbors called the Universe, but this is truly a remarkable gift to behold. There are those who will dispute the Bible's declaration of God's creative powers and say that the world was created out of some cosmic bang, or seismic explosion. But, how does such a universal harmony that we experience in nature in the natural world come from something as violent and chaotic as an explosion? Everything in nature and in our world points to the Creationism of God, but mankind continues to refute it because of their disbelief not just in creation but the existence of God. However, every time you look at nature you see God, every time you look at the statuesque oaks and pines in the forest, and the quietly flowing streams and rivers, and the enormous and prestigious oceans and seas in geography, you are seeing the immense handiwork of God, the Creator of All Things. It took immense vision to speak a world into existence that never was created until He did it. He had nothing to go on but His on infinite intelligence, which was well suited for the task. The ability to create something from nothing, takes an enormous imagination and unimaginable brilliance that only God uniquely possess. As He saw He spoke and as He spoke He saw what He had originally seen before He spoke. So, things were happening instantaneously; as He saw, then He spoke and when He spoke things begin to happen. Geography and landscape begin to take shape at the ferocity and veracity of the Creator's own spoken word. Life begin to emerge out of nothing but the sheer will and vision of the

Creator. He spoke it and it was there, He said, "Let there be" and it was so. What a simple and yet magnificent display of the awesome power of God. Just like the prolific paint brush of Michelangelo whose sainted hands painted the Sistine Chapel, God willed the world into existence through the power of His own words. The magnificence of this enterprise is breathtaking to imagine, and would have been utterly spectacular to behold. And, vision was the completed world in the mind of God before He ever spoke one single word. Vision is not only the completed world in the mind of God, but the confidence in His capacity to bring what He saw from concept to reality. The creativity of God was and is seen in the vastness and depth of His creation. The creation of the world is validation of not just our existence but our purpose, we are here because we are supposed to be here. We are here, because someone thought we were important enough to be here, we are here because someone thought we were significant; that we were special; that the world that He created would not be complete without us being here. Subsequently, if all this was done before we got here and we are here, then everything around us should tell us that I am supposed to be here. There is nothing about my life that is coincidental, there is nothing about my life that is accidental or inconsequential but everything in my life happened for a purpose.

Vision Is a Gift from God

Vision is a gift from God; the ability to get a glimpse into the potential God deposited into you before you were formed is truly a gift. Essentially, vision is the ability to see what God sees when He looks at you. Vision continues to validate your purpose, because it serves as a visual interpretation of God's thoughts about you. Jeremiah 29: 11 declares, (KJV) "For I know the thoughts that I think towards you, saith God. Thoughts of good and not of evil to give you an expected end." This verse dispels the age-old myths about this overpowering ferocious being we call God, who wants nothing but to kill us or to destroy us. Conversely, this scripture in Jeremiah lets us know unequivocally that God has good thoughts about us and if God has good thoughts about us then that must mean that our lives are shrouded in purpose. If God wants nothing but the best for us, then why shouldn't we want anything less for ourselves? If God wants nothing but the best for us, then why are there so many people living beneath their privilege? Vision shows us what we can be, what we can do and what we can become, but in order to do it we have got to stick with the source. Vision only becomes a reality through Christ; it is a gift from God and it is materialized by God.

How can two people looking at the same thing both have two different descriptions of what they've seen? A perfect example of this is two eye-witnesses to a crime and both have two different descriptions of the suspect as well as what happened. How is this so, when the same occurrence transpired in front of both eye-witnesses, but they still end up with different perspectives of what happened? This could be so for a number of different reasons, maybe the 1st eye-witness only saw part of the crime, and the 2nd eye-witness saw the whole thing? Or, maybe they both saw the crime transpire, but were standing in two different places so their visual perspectives were very different. So, in essence, proximity and opportunity are two determining factors in the two-people seeing the same thing and both walking away with two different explanations of what happened. Such is the case when understanding the significance of having a vision, because two people could both be literally and figuratively looking at the same situation and both walk away with two completely different perceptions of reality. Two people could both be looking at a desert wasteland and one only sees the wasteland and the other sees a thriving community of real estate, retail, and industry. The two people both were looking at the same geography; the same location; the same space, but only one saw potential and promise where the other saw destituteness and decadence. Their natural vision is not what's being called into question, because they both saw the exact same desert wasteland, but something within them caused them both to have different perceptions of what they both saw. Essentially, this difference in perception is more of an estimation of one's own abilities, capabilities and the like rather than just a mere statement of potential in what they both saw. So the "excavationist" who saw enormous potential in what the prognosticator called a desolate wasteland essentially says more about the self-esteem of the two interlocutors than the potential or lack thereof in the desert land.

What is the reason for this disconnect? Why couldn't both individuals who physically saw the same thing also perceptually internalize the same thing? One could argue that this is why we each are unique, in that we are not all the same. We think differently, we act differently, we speak differently, and we ultimately see differently. Could it be the magnitude of our differences that have caused us to ultimately view everything else differently? Inasmuch as no one person is the same, how should we expect two people to see the same thing both in the same way? This appears to be an inner will or resolve that causes one to see things differently and because we view things differently we tend to react and respond to things differently as well. We've all heard of the proverbial glass half full, glass half empty analogy, which essentially separates the optimist from the pessimists, and this is basically the same principle being applied in our earlier analogy of two people viewing the same circumstances very differently. However, we are saying that people typically see things differently because they are inherently different, but there is another force at work that causes some people, to see what others cannot. What is this force the causes some people to see what others cannot? Where does this power come from? How does one obtain it? We believe this power is divinely given and the giver is God-himself, and we are the recipients of this tremendous gift of vision. To see what others cannot is an extremely powerful ability and one; that if properly executed, could yield tremendous benefits to those fortunate enough to have this valuable power.

The Blind Leading the Blind

What is interesting about us is that we believe our limited view of the world, and our limited view of life is sufficient to not just veil our blindness to others but appear to be sighted. In fact, we believe our limited sight or insight is not so limited. How could this be, when our minds are finite or our vision is limited; so, all we end up doing is trusting ourselves instead of the one who knows the way. And, the one who truly "knows" the way is the last one we seek for counsel or advice. Our lives are too important to live "thinking" our way through it, instead of "trusting" the one who "knows" the way. And the unfortunate part about this perception or misperception, or both is that we don't know that we don't know and we are often the last ones to admit we don't know that we don't know. Although, our life's experiences have shown us that we don't know the way, but we're too stubborn to admit we don't know what we're doing. We just want the right to chart our own course and when it ultimately fails we also want the right to not have to accept responsibility for charting the wrong course. Not realizing that the only person that we're hurting throughout this entire process, is also the same person that is convinced they know what they're doing. What a conundrum!

I know you've heard the saying, "the blind leading the blind they both fall in the ditch." While the analysis of this scenario may seem a bit troubling, yet is a very teachable moment for those of us who are looking for answers to life's questions about our purpose. Firstly, if both individuals are blind, what qualifies either of them to lead the other? They both share the same physical condition and yet one of them still feels like they're able to lead them both in the right direction. Secondly, it seems that both individuals are unwilling to admit that they can't see, because it doesn't appear that either of them knows that they both can't see. And, no one is willing to admit the truth about their condition, the probability of their safe arrival at their pre-determined destination falls dramatically because of this sad reality. If no one is willing to deal with the truth of their condition, it begs the question what is the real objective of them trying to lead each other. It seems; at least through the context of the quote, that they both think that the other person can see and therein lies the willingness to trust the other person's direction over their own. And, so it appears that the two blind individuals are not only lying to one another, but they're also lying to themselves about their inability to see the way. Therefore, the expected consequence of this futile endeavor is for them to both fall in the ditch. This seems like a rather fair consequence given their unwillingness to share the truth of their physical condition with one another. Whether it's out sheer stubbornness or trickery the end result is a fair exchange for this futile endeavor.

The larger point behind the analysis of this infamous scenario, is to emphasize the stubbornness of the blind men to admit not just to one another but even to themselves that their vision is impaired. Lying to ourselves has got to be at the top of the list of obstructions to us seeing clearly. Our unwillingness to admit to ourselves the truth about our mental and spiritual condition; in other words, denying that there is a problem really is the problem. Shakespeare said it best, " …to thy own self be true." If there is one person that we can ill-afford to be untruthful with it has to be with ourselves. We cannot continue to lie to ourselves and expect that things are going to automatically get better. Having a vision is not refusing to come to grips with the dark reality that is in front of us. Having a vision is accepting the dark reality in front of you, but choosing to see a brighter day ahead of you. In many ways, we've allowed our own stubbornness to stand in the way of our success.

I think when the truth is the starting point of this exchange, the end result will more than likely be different. It's one thing when you are unwilling to admit the truth to someone else, but it's an entirely different thing altogether when you are unwilling to admit the truth to yourself. Your vision may not be naturally impaired, but your mental vision might be impaired by what you are seeing naturally. Your natural eyes see dilapidation, poverty, crime ridden streets, and violence, which mentally translates into hopelessness, destruction, dead end and no way out. It's difficult to see hope when you are surrounded by hopelessness. Although, your perception seemed to accurately project what you naturally see, how do you rise above a seemingly insurmountable mental picture when nothing around you says that you can? Naturally, vision can be easily manipulated; what you see can easily be manipulated. You can see one thing and actually something entirely different is going on. That's called a diversion. In life, what you realize is that seeing clearly has absolutely nothing to do with our natural vision, but has everything to do with our mental and most importantly our spiritual vision.

CHAPTER 7

THE POWER OF VISION

"Action without vision is passing time, vision without action is merely daydreaming but vision with action can change the world."
— *Nelson Mandela*

Nelson Mandela was truly a man of action; embodying the essence of the opening quote we appropriately chose for this chapter. He was a visionary and a revolutionary; the two go hand in hand. Not only did Mandela envision a free South Africa, he spent his entire life making sure that what he saw became a reality. Herein lies the power of vision. It's one thing to see something and never take action; of which Mandela considers passing time or merely daydreaming, but when you couple action with vision you have the power to change the world. In Mandela's case, he had the power to change his world-South Africa. South Africa is the 25th largest country in the world, with a population of over 56 million people. Apartheid had plagued South Africa for almost five decades. In fact, Mandela was born into this institutionalized racist system;

even coming from royalty, he still experienced the brunt of this racist culture from a child to a young man. Even though he was born into this racist culture, one wonders if how you are exposed to a racist culture determines how you will ultimately respond to it? Does being born into a racist system make you more prone or less prone to eventually accept or reject the tenets of the culture? Or, does having the system itself thrusts upon you make you more resistant or less resistant? Personally, I believe it is ultimately driven by the individual; even though there may be many other factors at play, the person usually determines through their own volition whether they will resist or succumb to the pressures of institutionalization. Mandela never succumb to this system of segregation and discrimination, because it appeared to have never been in his nature to accept the status quo. Maybe it was his royal pedigree, but as you read the history of his life one can't help but to notice that Mandela was a revolutionary at his core. It is not uncommon for some people who were born into a system of institutionalized racism and discrimination to eventually become institutionalized themselves. Walking, talking marginalized representatives of the racist culture they are heavily exposed to. They voluntarily and even involuntarily carry the venomous racist culture with them wherever they go. It is embedded in their thoughts, their conversation, their behavior and attitudes, which in turn translates into their lifestyles as well.

The New Normal

What is dangerous about the Apartheid or institutionalized racism and segregation is when this system becomes normalized amongst the very people it was designed to oppress. When the very people the system was designed to oppress become numb to the vitriol and the evil that this racist culture projects, and act as though it is just a regular part of life, this is when the system of racism is most dangerous. This is when this culture is the most dangerous, because it is the less apt to change. If the people who the system is designed to oppress essentially do not oppose being oppressed, then there is no need for the system to change. When separate public restrooms and separate restaurant entrances are accepted as normal; when separate areas for seating on public transportation become just another part of their daily commute, then the real damage of Apartheid has already been done. Inasmuch as now the racist laws and segregationists polices have moved from the natural to the physiological, this is more damaging than the racists and policies themselves. Now the people have subconsciously accepted their own inferiority and their oppressor's superiority. And, this is what Apartheid was designed to accomplish, for it not just to create two separate societies but two separate classes of people both readily accepting their institutionalized roles. The interesting part is that the white oppressor who is ultimately responsible for the implementation of this racist system came into this enterprise voluntarily while the oppressed were involuntary institutionalized, but the end result is still the same, because you now have one race believing their superior by choice and the other believing their inferior by virtue of the system. So, for many South Africans the Apartheid became their new normal. Many were born into this racist belief system and subsequently knew nothing different. They were propagandized and marginalized from birth into believing they were inferior and their white oppressors were superior. Children being taught by their parents not to resist for fear of them being killed; essentially growing up involuntary accepting this racist system as a part of their way of life. It is extremely difficult for young children to grow up having to suppress their inherent will to rebel against the Apartheid partly because they were told by their parents not to, especially when the consequences of their rebellion could cost them their life. For some over time, their suppression ultimately became submission, which further perpetuated the evils of this system upon yet another vulnerable generation. Their suppressed rebellious desires were incubated for so long that they actually were abated, and what replaced those rebellious desires was complete and utter submission. People that were oppressed for so long by the ruling class and influenced by their own people to resist the will to rebel eventually produced docile subservient slaves; who's will was broken by the very people the system was designed to oppress.

And the same was so for the oppressors as well. Some were born into this system instilled within them the belief that they are the superior race of people. Within their own circles; the oppressed belief system was cultivated, the white oppressor instilled into their children and their children's children this corrupted belief system of superior and inferior people. White parents teaching their children that they are better than their South African counterparts. Parents who indoctrinated their offspring into believing they were indeed superior and those "dark-skinned" people were inferior. The ruling class would use all kinds of methods to indoctrinate the masses regarding this vicious belief system. Everything from public beatings, and killings to even using the Bible as a weapon against the African natives. Just like the slave owners of the South, the ruling class in South Africa used the Bible to justify their egregious beliefs in superior and inferior races. So, it was quite clear what Nelson Mandela would be up against when he made the conscious decision that he would be a life-long dissenter to this evil and wicked government of systematic racism. Mandela's philosophical approach to revolutionary change was that the system may not change overnight, but constant, deliberate resistance will continue to eat away at the system as well as win more support from the masses. Inasmuch as he knew that it is only when the people do not believe they deserve to be oppressed; it is only when the people believe that institutionalized racism and discrimination is wrong that the potential for the system to change, because the will of the people has changed. Mandela ultimately needed the support of the people in order for this victory over Apartheid to be won. The same is such for those budding visionaries who dare to see the world differently than the way it is. This is the context from which every visionary grapples to birth their vision; the way the world is and the way that it should be. Let's be clear, we are in no way asserting that those responsible for the implementation of this vicious system called the Apartheid are in some way visionary's because they dared to see the world differently than the way it was. They might consider themselves visionaries but we do not nor do we condone such a vicious system of government. We are simply identifying the power struggle that exist within any narrative where change is thought to be in order. One should automatically expect a rebellion of some kind, acceptance from some, as well as keepers of the status quo; of which we plan to discuss in greater detail later.

If Only They Knew

When you examine the mental damage that had been done to the mind of the oppressed, to have once rebelled against the system to no avail, but through the crucible of time they have come to accept their own inferiority. What a damaged person indeed. I'm reminded of the quote from the famous abolitionist Harriet Tubman; who when asked to give an estimate of the number of slaves she was able to free by way of the Underground Railroad, she said, "I freed a thousand slaves. I could have freed a thousand more if only they knew they were slaves" What an extremely profound and yet very telling indictment of the thousand or more slaves that could have been freed if only they knew they were slaves. This declaration coming from this great Abolitionist, which speaks to the degree of mental damage that had been done over and above the physical abuse that slaves endured each day on the plantations of the South. What Harriet was saying in essence is that the primary reason she couldn't free more slaves is because more of them didn't believe they actually were slaves. They believed they were a part of the family, they believed they were inherently inferior to the white slave masters, they believed the slaves masters cared about their well-being. If only they knew they were slaves they would have believed they deserved to be free; if only they knew they were slaves they would know they were not supposed to be beaten and brutalized; if only they knew they were slaves they would know they were not inherently inferior; if they knew they were slaves they would be more willing to escape, if they knew they were slaves there would have been more of an innate resistance to being enslaved. So, in order for someone to experience freedom they must first realize they are a slave. Here we can see the results of the mental slavery that was at work, which was far more impactful than any physical abuse the slaves could have ever received.

Harriet Tubman had to realize in her quest for freedom that you can't save everybody. Even though every slave on that plantation whether they were in the field or in the house was worthy of freedom and deserving of it, everyone didn't want to go through it what it takes to be free. Every slave didn't want to have to escape during the night, sometimes leaving family and friends behind; leaving others who didn't believe escaping was the solution nor was it even possible. This is the kinds of people that a determined Harriet Tubman had to contend with. And, you can almost see the determination in her eyes in photos and pictures that we've seen of her, which may have been an indication of the kind of person that she was, or the person she believed she had to be in order to survive. She was the epitome of "no none sense." I'm only taking those who truly want to be free with me. If you don't want to be free or if you're vacillating between two opinions then you can't go. It's all or nothing, either you want to be free or you want to be enslaved, you choose.

Such as it is with prospective visionaries who dare to see the world differently than the way it is. You considered too idealistic, too naïve, too far-fetched. You are constantly being reminded that change in almost impossible. It takes too much effort; it's far too risky, it will take too much work; it's not worth it. Your idealism is viewed as too risky. However, isn't this usually how new vision is reacted to by those on the outside looking in? Vision is groundbreaking; vision is game changing, vision is a shock to the system. You should expect resistance and opposition from those who don't see what you see, that should be considered a normal part of the visionary discipline. It should be your expectation to encounter naysayers and haters. You should expect to run into those who don't see things the way you do. After all, you are the one with the vision, and everybody will not see things the way you do. Everybody doesn't have a visionary spirit; everyone doesn't have the capacity to be receptive to ideas and concepts they can't see themselves. This is the very definition of "small-minded" people, of which you most certainly encounter during your pursuit of fulfillment. This is why there are less leaders and more followers, this is why there are less shepherds and more sheep. You should probably consider this as almost a rite of passage. But, you must continue to forge ahead, and don't' allow yourself to get distracted or overwhelmed by those who don't see things the way you do.

The Keepers Vs. The Visionaries

So, when you juxtapose the dangers of the normalization of the Apartheid and the realization of the slave's actual slavery, you can see how critical perception becomes in helping to understand why some remain slaves and others fight for their freedom. You can even see how in the context of our vision theme why visionaries sometimes get pushback from those who we will refer to as the "Keepers of the Status Quo" inasmuch as they don't see "eye to eye" on the visionary's new view of their world. This is a very interesting dynamic taking place between these two very different kinds of people because there are two distinct ideologies at play; the way the world is and the way it should be. Before we discuss the profile of the visionary, we would first like to discuss the Keepers of The Status Quo, for they provide us with insight into the lives of those who prefer to keep things the way they are. The Keepers of the Status Quo are usually people who are extremely close-minded, pessimistic-optimism; there is a weird optimism embedded within their pessimistic thought process that if they don't upset the "apple cart" if they don't upset the equilibrium of the system or the balance of power, things have a way of taking care of themselves. This is the mentality of the "Keepers" The Keepers are the quasi slaves on the plantation or as they were often called, The Uncle Tom's or the "House Negro's". They believed in the master's way of doing things, they not only believed in the system but they defended it. The Keepers strongly believed that their livelihood was somehow directly tied to the sustainability of this racist system. Malcolm X described this type in a speech he gave at Michigan State University in January of 1963. In this speech Malcolm was essentially identifying the primary differences in the two different types of slaves that worked on the plantations in the South one was the "House Negro" and the other was the "Field Negro." They both lived very

different lives on the plantation, primarily because of their proximity to the master or the slave owner. And, their proximity to the master was essentially determined by their relationship to the master. For our purposes, the "House Negro" is the same as the "Keepers" which are the defenders of the status quo and they will do what it takes defend the status quo because they see that their destinies are somehow intertwined. Malcolm X went so far as to say of the "House Negro" that are their lives were so intertwined with their master's, *"when the master would be sick, the house Negro identified so much with the master that he would say, what's the matter boss we sick?"*

And, this in essence, is how acquainted the house Negro would become with the master that he mimics his master's pain just to stay in his good graces. Likewise, the Keepers of the status quo will mimic the very thing that continues to keep them in bondage just to avoid from having to get out and explore new territory or to try something new. You have people who are so insecure in themselves that the only way they can find comfort in their misfortune is to berate and ridicule the ones who are willing to step outside of their comfort zone and try something new. What they are attempting to do is to bring the visionary down to their level so they can now share the same space of inferior thinking. In a sense, the Keepers have adopted the characteristic of the very thing that is oppressing them as a way to insulate them from the people who are willing to look at the world with a fresh perspective or vantage point. And, it also serves as a readymade excuse to not doing anything or be anything more than what they already are. This destructive behavior prompted famed author and motivational speaker Les Brown to conclude "no one can rise from to expectations."

This was the mentality of the house Negro-according to Malcom X; who in some ways mirrors some of the same characteristics of the Keeper. They have become the walking and talking embodiment of their oppressor, which in this case is the status quo. They are an enemy of change and absolutely see no need for it. They are the ones who constantly say, "this is the way it always was and this is the way it always should be." But, what they are saying in a sense is that stagnation is better than progress. And stagnation is not just an enemy of progress it is also an enemy of change, which is one of the key components of vision. Change is an inevitability of life; it is a reality that all of us have to deal with. However, when you hear the musings of the Keeper you get a glimpse of the mental slavery they have become imprisoned by. They have forgone their own physical and mental independence to become the complete and total responsibility of someone else. Why, because they have convinced themselves that things are better the way they are.

Conversely, the lifestyle of the visionary is always different than everybody else. They walk differently, they dress differently, their attitude and behavior is different. The desire to fit in or to be liked doesn't exist for the visionary, because they are not trying to fit in; they understand they were born as the song writer Tye Tribett so pointedly declared, "To Stand Out." The visionary can be characterized as Malcolm X described in the same speech he delivered at Michigan State in Jan of 1963 as the field Negro, who he says,

"the field negro was the masses. They were in the majority. When the master got sick, they prayed he'd die. When the house caught on fire, they'd pray for a wind to come along and fan the flames."

The field Negro in many ways represents the lifestyle of the visionary, because while working out in the field they never lose sight of who they were. They always remembered their truest identity, they're job was different, their mentality was different, they're perspective was different, their attitude was different. Not just because of where they worked in contrast to where the house Negro worked, but because what they saw was different. They saw the strength of their brothers and sisters in the cotton fields, they saw their courage and determination, they saw their will to survive, they saw outward rebellion against this vicious system. And, because of what they saw in front of them, they were also able to see a better day ahead of them; because of what they saw in the cotton fields of the South, gave them courage to escape through the Underground Railroad headed North, because of the brutality and violence they saw from the slave masters, they could see the day where they were no longer anybody's slave.

The Visionary vs The Apartheid

The dynamic between the Visionary's and the Keeper's is interesting, because there is a constant ideological friction between what is and what should be. And when you apply this dynamic to the context of the Apartheid in South Africa, you really begin to see what Nelson Mandela was up against in eliminating this vicious system. It wasn't just the ruling party he had to deal with, but now it was the Keepers from within his own people that wanted to keep things the way they were. The Keepers wanted to maintain the status quo for many different reasons; some people thought change was impossible; it would be too hard to overthrow the white ruling class because they had too much money, power and influence to keep the system in place. Others wanted to keep the system because it was all they knew and they had learned to survive and even thrive in this perverse culture of systematic racism. Some even looked at Mandela and others like him as troublemakers, because they were always somewhere inciting riots having public demonstrations and protest, which; in the minds of the Keeper, did more harm than good. The problem with all of these is that they were coming from the very people the system itself was designed to oppress and they wanted it to remain. One would've hope that the negative impact from the Apartheid would've created a uniform dissenting force of South Africans rather than a divided country of not just the oppressor vs the oppressed but now some of the oppressed populous have ventured over to the oppressor's side of history. So, this is the dynamic that Mandela and others like him were up against. It's one thing for you to be fighting an enemy of another race, ethnicity, belief system, etc. but it is another thing entirely to be fighting people that look just like you. What the ruling class did was recruit from within the ranks of the oppressed to police their own people. So instead of seeing white police officers patrolling the streets of South Africa, you see black South Africans policing other black South Africans. What an interesting dynamic. This is a page right out of the textbook of slavery, where the white slave masters would many times send their own black slaves that had been successfully institutionalized to capture and return escaped blacks slaves to the plantation. Historically, blacks have been accessories to their own demise; used as tools of the white oppressor to subdue and control their own black brothers and sisters. What a travesty; what a sinister plan of control and domination. And the sad part about all of this is that we were willing participants in the destruction of our own people. This is a dynamic that Mandela was up against. And it is from this dynamic that we are able to really see the power or the impact of vision, because in order for Mandela- the revolutionist visionary, to topple the authoritarian government of the Apartheid and free South Africa, he not only had to go through the ruling class but he also to go through his own people to reach that goal. Mandela sacrificed 27yrs of his own life in a Robbins Island prison and then in Pollsmoor Prison, where he would continue to dream and visualize a free South Africa. Mandela saw his resistance as revolutionary and directly in-line with the vision he saw for a free South Africa. He believed that non-violent and even violent resistance would be the catalyst for change that was needed to rid this country of this racist and segregationist system.

What Are You Willing to Do?

As a visionary, you have to be willing to risk somethings and sacrifice somethings in order to see your vision fulfilled. In fact, the passion for your vision must be reflected in your courage and determination to bring it from concept to reality. The question then becomes what are you willing to do to make it happen? What are you willing to sacrifice; what are you willing to give up? What are you willing to go without? What are willing to withstand? It is times like these where your internal acumen is really tested. You not only have to consider what you are willing to go without to see your vision accomplished but what are you not willing to let go of; what are you unwilling to compromise? What is non-negotiable? The answers to this question really reflects the intestinal fortitude that you possess to stand up to criticism, doubt, controversy and any other thing that will be thrown your way to thwart the fulfillment of your vision or dream. Your ability to stand up against criticism in some ways reflect the size and the magnitude of the vision, because your willingness to fight for your vision means that is worth the bumps and bruises you will encounter to get there.

You got to be willing to sacrifice for your vision, you have got to be willing to roll up your sleeves and get into the trenches if need be, because the worth of the vision is found in the tenacity of the visionary. However, determined you are is an indication of the value of the vision. Many have struggled, sacrificed and even died to ensure the posterity of their vision. We talked in Chapter 2 how Abraham died never seeing the actual fulfillment of God's promise to him that he would make his name great and his offspring would be the as large as the sands on the seashore. But, Abraham had enough faith in God to believe in its completion even though he wasn't alive to see it come to pass. The question remains, what are you willing to put up with, what are you willing to endure, what are you willing to fight for, the answers will again determine not just the value of vision but the tenacity of the visionary. Do you have what it takes to make it happen? Above of all else, you must believe that your vision or dream is worth the sweat equity it's going to take to bring into reality. If you believe it's worth it than your attitude, your behavior, your demeanor will all reflect the value you see in your vision. You've got to be able to see it before anybody else sees it. You've got to believe it before anybody else believes it; you've got to fight for it before anybody else will see that your vision is worth fighting for.

What Are You Made Of?

In a real sense, this process is as much about you as it is as much about the fulfillment of your vision. This is where you really find out who you are; this where you find out how strong you are; how much endurance you have, how much criticism you can handle, because anything worth having you are going to have to work for it. And it is during this process that you discover who you really are. It had been said that "you don't know how strong a roof is until rains" and likewise you don't know how much power you have until you have to use it. You are stronger then you think, you have more power then you realize, you can take more than you think. We consistently underestimate and undervalue ourselves when it comes to matters of the heart, but you were created to do more, you were created to handle more, you were created to be more. So, we need to embrace our more and walk in our more and use the examples of these powerful men and women of history to glean from and learn from to see your dreams and visions come to pass.

The fulfillment of your dream and vision in and of itself is indeed an accomplishment, but in the process, you also discover your own identity as well, which is just as important. Discovering your strengths and weakness throughout the process is what helps to mold and shape you into a true leader. Remember, the vision is not just for you to accomplish but it is for the people it was divinely ordained to impact.

Returning to our revolutionist visionary Nelson Mandela we see through the lens of history the steps he was willing to take to see Apartheid eradicated and to see a free South Africa. Spending most of his adult life behind bars, because he was so determined to not let Apartheid be the swan song of "his-story." History indeed tells us that he was determined, that he was indeed courageous, that he became the walking and talking embodiment of the vision he saw for his native land. History tell us that he was unrelenting in his quest for freedom for all of South Africa. Mandela also became an embodiment of his own words regarding vision, because he wasn't satisfied just dreaming about it, he wasn't satisfied just thinking about it, he wasn't satisfied until he started doing something about it. You can't just sit around and daydream about what you want to do or want you want to accomplish, but you've got to get out there and do something about it. Think about the countless amount of people that lived and died never accomplishing their dreams or visions. Think about the million-dollar ideas that died with the dreamer, because they never dared to step out there and give their vision a try. This can't be you, you can't let your opportunity pass you by, you were created for this. You were born for this, you were created for greatness. You are the answer to the problem the world's been waiting to solve.

In Your Dreams

I'm reminded of a speech that I wrote for a Middle School Promotional Ceremony that was entitled "In Your Dreams." The premise behind this speech was to take this familiar derogatory phrase that was often used among adolescents as a put down to someone who had expressed a dream or a goal they would like to achieve. The response many times from their peers would be an emphatic, "*i*n your dreams!" We endeavored to switch that derogatory phrase into a positive admonition that would encourage our young people to continue to think big, continue to dream, continue to believe in the impossible. We began by saying,

"*You are the young people that will lead this world further then it had ever been before. You will accomplish things that scientists and engineers are only contemplating and thinking about now. You will go places that many have never gone before, you will see things that your parents have never seen. You will accomplish things that have only been dreamed of. The world has been anxiously awaiting your arrival. The future of the world hangs in the balance as it anticipates the tremendous impact you are going to make ...*

We concluded the speech by saying,

In your dreams, lies the solution to world hunger
In your dreams, lies the cure for cancer
In your dreams, we catch a glimpse of tomorrow
In your dreams is the location of your success
In your dreams, we find the answer to world peace
In your dreams, we discovered uncharted territory
In your dreams, we see the next Michael Jordan
In your dreams, we see the next Lebron James
In your dreams, we see the next Williams Sisters
In your dreams, wee the next Tiger Woods
In your dreams, lives will be changed
In your dreams, no will be left behind
In your dreams racism, and classicism do not exist ...
   ... Everyone will know the world only became better because it lived in your dreams."

This is an excerpt of a speech we often gave at graduations and promotional ceremonies, because it was designed to motivate the next generation of young people to continue to dream. Regardless of how much negativity you are confronted with, regardless of how dark and bleak your environment maybe, regardless of how hopeless life may seem for you, never stop dreaming. Never stop seeing yourself living better; doing better, having better. You are worth the investment; you are worth the time and the energy. These are the kinds of things our youth today need to hear; these are the types of affirmations that need to be rehearsed in their schools; these are the types of things that need to be said in our homes. If we want to see our young people achieve better we have got to continue to challenge them to do better. Our youth will only rise to the expectations we have for them and if they are not being challenged or there is no one there to challenge them then we only have ourselves to blame when they end up nothing more than minimum wage earners or street pharmacists, prison dwellers, or even worse still-pushing up daisies. The flip side of that coin is that we have to be better role models and better positive examples in the lives of this next generation of young people. We cannot ask more of them than we are willing to give ourselves. The reality is there currently is a shortage of positive role models in our society and unfortunately the role models they have are setting the wrong example for them and leading them down the wrong path. We have to do a better job at cultivating and grooming the next generation of young leaders. Doing this today will ensure we will have a better tomorrow. We can't continue pointing the finger at one another or playing "the blame game" But our future; the world's future is housed in the vessels of the next generation, and investing in them today will certainly benefit us all tomorrow. This is a positive investment that is sure to reap huge dividends if the time is taken today to inspire an empower our future. We would be doing ourselves a tremendous disservice if something isn't done to save our youth. They are the hidden treasures and jewels of the world that needs to be polished and curated so they can shine bright like the diamonds they are.

The Rewards Are Great

Mandela, after spending most of his adult life in prison was released by then President of South Africa F.W. de Klerk. The ruling party released Mandela for fear of a civil war, and it was at this point that Mandela and de Klerk sat down to negotiate an end to Apartheid in South Africa. 27yrs after Mandela was arrested for revolting against the Apartheid, this racist system was disbanded by the very same party that put it in place. The process of independence had officially begun in Mandela's native land, and in 1994 South Africa had their first democratic election where he became President. Nelson Mandela and the African National Congress won the 1994 election and became the ruling party in South Africa. Mandela not only saw the end of Apartheid in his native country, but he also became the new leader of it as well.

What a tremendous reward for a man who sacrificed most of his life for the cause of freedom, not just for himself but for the 56 million South Africans that lived in this country. Mandela envisioned a day where every man, woman, boy and girl in his native country would have the same rights and privileges. He saw a day where everyone would have the same opportunities, where everyone would have the right to vote, where everyone would be treated with dignity and respect. And, that day finally came in 1994. With great sacrifice comes great rewards, because the same man that endured police beatings and brutality, the same man that endured malicious and unfair treatment for most of his adult life is now at the helm of leadership of the world's 25th largest nation. I remember seeing photos of South Africans waiting in long lines to elect Mandela as President. What a tremendously historic occasion, to have overcome one of the most vicious and racist systems the world has ever known to now being on the cusp of seeing his vision come into full view. This is where you can really see the power and the impact of vision. Mandela's vision was not just for himself, and the value behind it was not for his benefit alone, but it was for the millions of South Africans that would no longer be under a racist regime and now have freedom and equality as inherent rights and privileges of a democratic way of life.

The power of Mandela's vision was revealed through the lives of the millions of South Africans that were completely changed through his sacrifice and determination to not give in to racism and discrimination any longer. We can see the impact of Mandela's vision as he went from the squalor of a prison cell at Robbins Island; one of the most horrific prisons in the world, to the Presidency of South Africa. Whether this was Mandela's desire or not to lead South Africa remains to be seen; whether this was a part of Mandela's vision in the beginning to lead his native land, is not something we are here to debate. His hard work, courage and determination yielded huge dividends and brought about monumental change to a country that was in desperate need of change. I personally do not believe that the nation's presidency was one of Mandela's goals, because of the selflessness that he exhibited all throughout his life. The presidency itself; I believe, was South Africa's reward to their fearless champion. This office was a reward that the nation collectively gave to its greatest citizen for having the courage and intestinal fortitude to see his vision through until the end.

Mandela's example should resonate with all prospective visionary's regarding the power and the impact of vision. Vision is a powerful tool that when coupled with action can do as Mandela said, "change the world." There is no better person to utter those words than a man who is a prime example of what each word means. This paradigm of this entire country has now been changed, because one decided that his life was worth the sacrifice to change a nation. Your dreams and visions may not be on that grand of a scale, but whatever scale they are, invest your blood, sweat and tears into them because your vision is only as big as your commitment you make towards seeing it through. to see the value, you have to see the worth before anyone else will.

Chapter 8

VISION FOR THE
NEXT GENERATION

"And it shall come to pass in the last days that I will pour out my Spirit upon all flesh and your sons and daughters shall prophesy; and your young men shall see visions and your old men shall dream dreams"

- Acts 2:17

I remember one summer evening in April a few years back, my family and I were celebrating my mother's birthday. We had just eaten a really nice dinner at a restaurant and thought what better way to cap off the evening than a nice stroll Downtown Detroit at the Riverwalk. General Motors has made a considerable financial investment in the redevelopment of Downtown Detroit; particularly right behind the Renaissance Center which is now the General Motors Global Headquarters. People come from all over the city and its surrounding areas just to enjoy the scenery, and the beautiful view of the buildings of our Canadian neighbors cascading off the Detroit River in the ambience of the night's air. At the time, traveling with us was my two small children, my wife, my father and my mother. The evening was so tranquil and the weather was so warm and the scenery downtown by the Riverwalk was nice and inviting. We were really enjoying our time Downtown as a family. Oddly enough, this leisurely stroll took a very strange turn when as we were walking back in the direction of the parking structure where our vehicle was located, we saw a large group of people moving very rapidly in our direction. As they approached us, we were informed that there was a brief altercation between some teenagers down by the Renaissance Center. As a result, people were now being redirected by the police to leave the Riverfront area. We ended up having to take a slightly different route back to our car. As if that wasn't bad enough, as we get inside of the parking structure, shots rang out from just outside, which immediately sent everybody in the vicinity into a panic. My family began running towards my vehicle hurrying trying to get into the car and hopefully out of harm's way. Needless to say, we did everything that we could to get out of that parking structure as fast as we possibly could. Interestingly enough, that leisurely stroll that we decided to take quickly took a turn for the worst, and it came without warning and very little time to recover. The worst part about this story is not that our evening stroll was interrupted by senseless violence from some reckless teenagers. But, the worst part is the residual effects of this violent altercation and how it has impacted our future choices of activity and entertainment in the very same city I grew up in.

The Residual Effects of Teen Violence

It is sad when the climate of violence amongst our inner city and urban youth has become so impactful that it begins to narrow your choices of commerce, recreation, entertainment based in large part on the safety and security of the environment. I have to admit that I have personally chosen not to go certain places with my family, primarily because the location seems to be more conducive for violence than other places within the inner-city. Unfortunately, this is a regular occurrence for a lot of our inner-city and urban youth not just in Detroit but in Urban America. This is not out of the realm of possibility for a young boy who just wanted to play some pickup basketball at the neighborhood park, only to be cut down in the hail of gunfire because of a disagreement between rival street gangs. We have got to do something. We have got to change the trajectory of our youth. There is no way they should believe that violence is the only way to solve their problems. There is no reason why they should believe that indulging in drugs or other intoxicants is the only way to have a good time. There is no reason why they should believe that taking from someone else is the only way that could have something for themselves. Something has to be done.

Some of the more immediate residual effects of the teen violence in the inner city is of course matters of individual and collective safety. Events that take place in the city require a heavier police presence, because usually violence erupts in larger crowds. People usually make decisions about attendance of some of the grander events in Downtown Detroit based on this over-arching fact. For example, the Annual Fireworks that takes place the last Monday in June, usually draws somewhere between 1 million and 2 million people. So, you can imagine the congestion and the crowds in just every area downtown. Policing large crowds like these are an enormous task for the boys in blue, but they do the best job possible in making sure everyone has an enjoyable time. Over the years, things have gotten significantly better when coming downtown for larger events, but the concern for safety is still at the forefront of our minds.

There is also an economic impact of the effects of teen violence in the inner city and urban communities, not just in the Detroit area, but everywhere in Urban America. Teen violence usually takes place in some of the poorer dilapidated neighborhoods and communities in the inner-city, and because of the poor quality of life of many of the residents not much focus, or attention is given to these communities by the municipalities, the media and even the police. The presupposition is that the lack of money, and other resources implicitly suggests a lack of concern from not just the external mechanisms of the city, but an overall lack of concern internally from the residents who desperately need some help.

The Numbers Tell the Story

This generation is plague with so many problems; it seems, we are in what is a considered to be the "Golden Age" of technology. Everything is literally at your fingertips. You would think that this kind of access would produce some the most intelligent and brilliant minds this generation has ever seen. While this might be the case in small pockets around the country here and there, by and large the prevailing belief is it seems the more we have the less we have become. Statistics overwhelmingly show that the dropout rate far exceeds the graduation rate for inner city youth in record fashion. An Oct 11th Article in the Huffington Posts reports some startling statistics regarding the dropout rates of low income and minority students compared to their high-income counterparts.

"...4.8 % of blacks and 5.8 percent of Hispanics between 15 and 24 dropped out of grades 10-12, compared with 2.4 % for white students ... the dropout rate for low-income students was five times greater than their high-income counterparts — 7.4% compared with 1.4 %."

These are some very alarming statistics to say the least. The article also reported that,

"...the report's more disturbing discovery is that there were about 3 million 16- to 24-year-olds in October 2009 who were neither enrolled in high school nor had earned a high school diploma or alternative degree. These dropouts accounted for 8.1 percent of the 38 million U.S. non-institutionalized and civilians in that age group not in high school and without a high school credential."

It has been said many times when evaluating the plight of today's minority youth in comparison to the times of their forefathers and mothers, we; as a people, were more when we had less, and now that we have more we are so much less. Having more is what we thought we needed back in the 60's and 70's in order to be more. Our forefathers and mothers marched and fought for the generations that would follow would have more then what they had, with the belief that it would make the next generation better. The fact of the matter is, it has only made us exponentially worse. Now it seems that more we have, the more have access to, the worse we as a people have become. We have done less with more than our forefathers and foremothers ever would have done. History reminds of the accomplishments of our black ancestors who accomplished so much with so little. And, it would seem in our pursuit for more it would inevitably make us better. But, quite frankly it has only made us much worse. The moral decay, and lack of concern for our fellow man is extremely disturbing.

When considering all of this one has to wonder in who's hands are we entrusting the future of our world? What kind of future do we have to look forward to if the carriers of our future are as disproportionately disadvantaged and marginalized as they are. In who's hands are we placing the future of our communities? In who's hands are we entrusting to lead our school systems? In who's hands are we placing the keys to our municipalities and state legislatures?

But is it entirely the fault of our youth? Are they the ones that are to blame entirely for what they have ultimately become in our society? Does the blame of failing schools lie at the feet of our students? Are the dilapidated neighborhoods entirely the fault of its minority and low-income occupants? The answer is a resounding "No" on all fronts. The reality is the system itself is corrupt and the youth are just the by-products of a corrupt system. Unfortunately, today's youth are at the center of a power struggle between government and the educational system, and at the heart of the struggle isn't how are we going to properly educate our young people, but it is M-O-N-E-Y. I believe the Hip Hop Group- Wu Tang appropriately characterized the plight of the educational systems of our inner cities, "Cash Rules Everything Around Me ... Dollar, Dollar Bill Ya'll!" The education gap is widening more and more in our urban community's vs our suburban schools, more money is spent per student in the suburbs than in the inner city, and students from both geographical areas are given the same state exams with the same standards impressed upon both institutions and their students. It appears the odds are vehemently stacked against them. The expectations from the powers that be are for them to fail. Quite frankly, it is difficult to fathom how any student from the inner city is able to succeed in a system that seems so corrupt, and yet they do.

We hear success stories all the time about students who surpassed the odds and overcame obstacles and hurdles to achieve success even in a system that is so corrupt. We hear about students all the time who did not allow their environment to determine how far in life they would go, they refuse to allow themselves to be define by mediocrity and negativity. They refuse to succumb to the naysayers and prognosticators of our society who've already said they would never amount to anything. This is actually what it is going to take to be successful in the 21st Century. You cannot allow what you see around you to determine the vision that's in you. You have got to preserve despite the haters and spectators in your life who are standing on the sidelines waiting to see you fall. I wouldn't give them the satisfaction, if nothing else their hatred should be your incentive and motivation to continue.

Confused Generation

Another problem that is plaguing this generation of young people is that are completely and utterly confused about who they are. It is true that your teenage years are by far the most impressionable; they are the years where you are the most vulnerable. But nowadays it seems that we've taken this to the farthest extreme. Experimentation has become the excuse of every young person in this generation. "We have to try it at least once." There is no such thing as abstinence or discipline, it seems like it is just one giant "free for all" and everyone can just go for themselves. And, maybe some of this is a result of the freedom that young people are given nowadays vs twenty, or thirty or forty years ago, where parents were more stricter and elicited more discipline. There was no such thing as "Experimentation" in order to see if I like or not. Your parents were your moral compass, and they told you what to stay away from and not to be bothered with. Our parents outlined a moral code for our lives, they instilled into us what was "right" and what was "wrong." Nowadays, because of the rise in teen pregnancy and single parent homes, children are being raised with less discipline and given more freedom to ultimately raise themselves. Hence the condition of confusion that so many of our young people are dealing with, because of the absence of real parenting in today's homes.

"Confused" is a word that would best describe this generation of young people. Literally and figuratively, this generation seems more confused than previous generations when it comes to identity; their sexuality; their direction and outlook on life. This word; I believe adequately characterizes the plight of this generation. They are confused about so many different things; identity being one of "thee" most important. If you don't know who you are, how far can you expect to go in life? Young people dabbling in homosexuality and lesbianism, because they are "confused" about who they are and who they love. Somewhere along the lines we got off track and our youth are experimenting in areas they have absolutely no business. This is why; we-as parents, have to do a better job at covering our children. We cannot allow any and everything to come into their space. We need to surround our youth with positive influences, because they only reflect what they have been exposed to. Exposure is the truth serum of life, you are who you hang around; you are a reflection of your greatest influences. The Word of God reminds us as parents of our responsibility to our offspring when it says, "train up a child in the way he should go, and when he is old he shall not depart." In other words, parents with vision raised children with vision or parents with high expectations for their children raise children with high expectations for themselves.

"Next" vs "Now"

Some say that our young people make of the "Next" generation, however I beg to differ; they are the "Now" generation. They have been preconditioned to believe that because they are "next" that there is nothing they have to do in the interim but just wait for their turn. And in some cases, this is the fault of the older generation, because they were unwilling to give up their time in the spotlight for a younger less experienced group to follow them. So, the term "Next" was conveniently chosen as a means to quail the youth's desire to replace their older more seasoned counterparts.

From the perspective of the older generation, they will tell you that it took most of their life to get to this position of comfort or wealth or both and they are not ready to give that up. Therefore, it was convenient to refer to the group coming behind them as "The Next Generation." In fact, it made their pending transition seem more official by labeling them "Generation Next." Next was also a reflection of everyone's general belief in the inevitability of tomorrow. There is no real need for you now, you can wait until tomorrow and I guarantee you'll be next. The mortality rate amongst youth 10 or 15 years ago was lower than it is today. The life expectancy of our youth has fallen drastically sense the mid to early 90's. These numbers translated into an overall attitude and behavior of the general populous that because of all of these prevailing factors that our youth can sit this one out and just to be called in the game of life; there's plenty of time left.

However, times have completely changed today this is now a completely and utterly erroneous misnomer that we need to get rid of, inasmuch as it has taken the urgency out of our youth's necessity to be engaged in their community, their schools, their churches, and most importantly themselves. In this socioeconomic climate, there is no time to "wait" for anything. In fact, we must adopt a pro-active approach to everything. We need to be working on solutions to problems that haven't even materialized yet. This is how important and necessary the plight of today's youth is to the posterity of our communities, neighborhoods, schools, places of worship, and society as a whole.

We cannot afford to let them off the hook by giving them the excuse "Not now" but you are "Next." Times are far too severe, and young people are dying far too soon for us to continue to say that they are next. They may not be around to be next if we as a community don't do something for them now. Next suggests that tomorrow is guaranteed; next implies that we will be here tomorrow. Not so! Tomorrow isn't promised, so we have to live every moment as if it were our last. In fact, years ago being next meant that you had your whole life ahead of you. It meant that you could take your time and even be a little lazy when it comes to doing certain things. For example, I remember always cringing a bit when I was asked as a teenager what do I see myself doing 10 years from now. I didn't really know, but at the same time I didn't want to let on that I didn't know. So, I would give somewhat of a cookie-cutter answer, because I wanted to at least sound prepared even though I knew I wasn't. Those days are gone now. Time seems to be going by at an accelerated pace in these last days. And, being young doesn't have the sane meaning it had 20 or 30 years ago. Quite frankly, it doesn't have the same meaning it had when I was young.

Consequently, when we say this is the "Now" generation what we are saying in essence is that we cannot afford to take anything for granted. Life is far too precious, our young people far too important for us to shelve their future, because we don't believe it's there time yet. I say, tomorrow can't wait until we're ready, so we must spend the rest of today getting ready for tomorrow. I believe it is from our preparation that we find more confidence in a season that hasn't materialized yet. Constant preparation also translates into constant awareness. And the last thing that we want for the carriers of our future is for them to be completely unaware. Unaware and lack of preparation go hand in hand.

They cannot afford to be unaware of how they are going to pay for their college education, they cannot afford to be unaware that getting good grades in school is a must. They cannot afford to be unaware that hanging around the wrong people could cause irreparable damage to your future. They have to be, they must be prepared.

Much in the same way that the term "Now" speaks to preparation, it also speaks to another important word call proactivity. In these dangerous times we live in we not only cannot afford to be unaware or unprepared, but we have to become proactive. We as a society and even as a community have been conditioned to react to everything, which means most times when we react it is already too late, the damage has been done. But, for the sake of our future and the future of our young people, we can no longer be reactive but we must be proactive. Our future is far too important for us to continue reacting to problems that we should be collectively working on a solution. The future of our youth is far too important for us to still be reacting to teen violence instead of coming up with some viable solutions towards keeping our young people off the streets and in the classrooms or in the employment arena. We have to be about the business of giving our young people a new vision for themselves and their future. For too long they have succumbed to violence in their neighborhoods; for too long they succumb to the trappings of the drug world; for too long they have succumbed to the promiscuity of teen pregnancy. But today, the future of our young people is too important to continue venturing down the wrong path. We need more adults to stand up and roll up their sleeves and get in the trenches to save our young people. Their future is at stake; our future is at stake.

Who Is Ultimately Responsible?

As we watch the news and see story after story about our young people involved in criminal activity; senseless killings, robberies and murders, and just when you think you have heard it all they find another way to disturb you all over again. Something has to be done. The future of our communities is at stake; the future of our neighborhoods is at stake; the future of our schools is at stake; the future of our society is at stake. We have to begin the process of reprogramming our youth to believe they are more than thugs and gangsters, they are more than teenage parents, they are more than prison inmates, they are more than wasted space in a morgue. It has to start somewhere. We cannot continue watching our youth make bad decision after bad decision, because we become an accessory to their own demise. There has to be a reprogramming and reconditioning of the older generation. There must be a greater accountability that exists between the older generation and the younger generation. Both generations are directly and indirectly responsible to one another. The posterity of each generation depends heavily on the other. There has to be a meeting of the minds of some kind that can help us to get to a place of amicability and cooperation that will save our youth from imminent destruction.

Yet another reason we must help our youth is because when we help them, we help ourselves as well. When we help our youth, we ensure a brighter future for ourselves. When we help our youth, we are ensuring a safer community for ourselves. When we help our youth find employment, we are taking youth off the street and making them gainfully employed. When we help our youth, we are essentially reclaiming our neighborhoods and communities. We are becoming a part of the overall solution rather than a continued accessory to the problem.

The responsibility rests with us first to be better parents, nurturers, role models, examples to our youth than we have been. We cannot continue to expect so much from them and very little from ourselves. No longer can we continue pointing at them as if the problem of teen pregnancy originated with them. No longer can continue pointing the finger at them as if the problem of gang violence originated with their generation. No longer can we continue pointing the finger at them as if the problem of drug abuse originated with them. But, we have to commit to being better examples of "right living" for today's youth. They have to be able to see real life examples of good parenting; real life examples of fatherhood and motherhood in their communities. Our youth have to be able to see what a good father and mother looks like in person rather than just on television. They have to be able to reach out and touch a real-life doctor or lawyer rather than seeing them on their tv screen or sitting across from them in a courtroom or emergency room. This is not how our youth's first encounter with professional people in our society should be. Their first experience with a judge shouldn't be standing trial for a crime they committed in their community. Their first experience with a doctor shouldn't be because they contracted an STD during unprotected sex. However, these are the harsh realities that are youth are faced with every day. These are the everyday realities of today's youth that have become as routine and common as a cold. What a sad reality that our youth are faced with.

What Are Some Solutions?

We have to take a more "hands on" approach with our young people. These problems are not going to go away on their own, but we have to roll up our sleeves and commit ourselves to being a part of the solution rather than continue to proliferate the problem. The bold fact remains is that whether you are actively working against the solution or sitting on the sidelines, you are just as culpable and just as accountable. So, we cannot afford to use the excuse that it's not me, I will leave that for someone else to do. The times have become too severe for you to sit idly by and watch our youth be destroyed. There are really only two choices in the matter when it comes to saving our youth; either you are a part of the problem or you are a part of the solution. There is no in between there is no middle ground. The situation has become too dire and too severe for us to take a back seat any longer and say, "I'm going to sit this one out and let someone else handle it."

Another reason we can no longer stand on the sidelines and watch someone else do all the work is that there are far less people committed to helping our youth than the job itself requires. We can never say that we have enough people that are helping; we can never say that we have enough financial support from the government and municipalities; we can never say that we have enough manpower, because as long as new babies are being born without fathers, as long as new babies are being born in single parent homes, as long as new babies are being born to mothers on welfare, as long as new babies are being born to mothers without life insurance or healthcare the by-products of these larger problems will exist and the more help that is needed.

Giving Our Youth a New Vision

We have to give our youth a new vision of themselves, because the prognosticators of society have already institutionalized many of them before they even come out of their mother's womb. Inner city and urban youth are marginalized many times even before they are conceived. This is so, because there is a factor at play even before conception that will have a lasting negative impact on the lives of the offspring based solely on the ineptitude-ness of the carriers of the next generations seed. Essentially, the baby mothers and baby daddies of this next generation's behavior and actions are so severe that by the time the child is born they will already be exponentially further behind children who were born to more responsible and more productive parents. Children that are being born into a world they had nothing to do with are being asked to do more than they've been equipped to handle by the very same people that decided to bring them here. If something isn't done to subvert this process in some way by a concerned family member, or relative, or interested third party, this next generation will be completely extinct. Absent responsible parents in the lives of the next generation is one of the prevailing problems that continues to haunt these precious young people. Kids raising kids essentially is the reason why we see a lack of moral values, ethics, and a sense of responsibility in this generation. It is ultimately to our detriment and to the posterity of our future if we do not intervene in some way shape or form to help this wayward generation of young people.

It is so very important that our youth see a new vision of themselves, because what is in front of them is nothing but death and destruction. This new vision must not come from network television or a blockbuster movie. This new vision mustn't come from the next season of professional football or basketball, But, this new vision must be one that is up close and personal. This new vision must be one that they can reach out and touch; this new vision must be one that they can communicate with face to face. Essentially, what we're saying is that for too long success for our youth has only been seen through the camera lens of the television or the movie screen, which in some ways mystifies success and makes it seem so far removed from the dismal and bleak realities of their everyday lives. And, if our young people can only relate to successful people through what they see on television or in the movies, we can see why they are as hopeless and despondent as they are.

We need to change the paradigm of success, we need to make success more palatable, and more attainable in the minds of our youth. We have to begin to expose our young people to the success we expect them to have in the future. If we want them to be the next doctors and lawyers in our communities, then they need to be able to interact with these professionals on a personal level. And, we're not talking about a visit to the emergency room or as a companion in an interrogation room. But, our youth need to be able to reach out to them and to speak to them on a personal level. They need to be able to see that these people are real people; they are not so far removed from their reality that the occupations themselves are attainable. If the only interaction they have with a doctor is when they're being treated for a gunshot womb than we have serious problem. If the only interaction our youth have with the police is because of traffic stop then we have a serious problem. We have to begin to bridge the societal gap between the professional world and our young people. They need to be introduced and re-introduced to their future selves.

Give Them Back to God

Our youth are precious God- given jewels that we-as their guardians, have to protect and nurture. Inasmuch as we protect them we are protecting our future, as we nurture them we are nurturing our tomorrows; as we lead and guide them, we are in turn creating leaders that will lead the next generation into their future. The worst thing that we can do as a community is to turn our backs on our youth. In doing so, we will be ultimately turning our backs on our future. The past, the present and the future are inextricably tied together in; as Dr. King puts it, "a single garment of destiny." Each generation is responsible for the posterity and success of the preceding generation. What was done in the past prepares us for today, and what happens today will determine the landscape of tomorrow.

The scripture we chose to open this chapter with is actually found in both the Old and the New Testament. In the Old Testament, it is found in Joel 2:28-32 (KJV) and in the New Testament it is found in the book Acts 2:17 (KJV). The scripture is an indicator of the potential that rests within any individual that has an encounter with God. And so, as to not alienate any age group that could potentially interact with God, the writer in both passages specifically identifies both the young and the old men, and what could possibly happen as a result of this divine interaction. The impact of this encounter is different for each age group. The prophet Joel says, "your young men shall see visions and your old men shall dream dreams ..." The bottom line is that everyone that has an encounter with Jesus their life will never be the same again. In this scripture Luke; who is believed to be the writer of this book, declares that the young men shall see visions, and notice he was careful to insert the word "see" into his pronouncement of their special abilities. Inasmuch as they now have a relationship with God they now have the capacity to see what could not ordinarily be seen. Our young men can now see a future that was hidden behind the dark lens of bondage. Now they are able to see a vision for themselves when before they were mentally and spiritually blind. An encounter with Jesus Christ is truly the antidote that the youth of this generation and succeeding generations need to be able to see themselves in a way they have never seen before. Giving our youth back to God is the answer to all of our societal problems. Giving them back to God in the same way, our newborns are christened at the altar of our churches across the globe, our youth must be given back to the God who gave them to us.

Christ indeed comes to set us free. He comes to free our vision; He comes to gives us a clear view of ourselves through His lens of success and not failure. When our youth are given vision from God they are truly able to see themselves as God sees them. From a liberated perspective, they can only see what God sees when He looks at them and how valuable they really and truly are, but they can also see the plot of the enemy against them. Our youth's immense value to God is attractive to the enemy. Their value is directly and indirectly tied to the purpose God has divinely given to each and every one of them. The enemy knows that whatever God places value on is destined for greatness. This is why, the devil has had an adversarial pursuit on the future of young people. He knows that if he can stop them, he can stop the future, if he can stop the youth than he can stop tomorrow, if he can stop the youth, then he can utterly destroy mankind. This is how important and significant and critical our young people are in determining the architecture of tomorrow.

When they were blinded by the devil they could not see their immense value, they could not see their divine purpose. But, now that their mental and spiritual sight have been liberated, they can not only see their value, but they can now see the enemy for who he truly is. You can now see why the devil wanted you blinded in the first place. Now that your sight has been officially liberated, you can see your enormous potential, you can see how your purpose has been insulated from the traps of the enemy. Now that your sight has been liberated, you can truly see as the Apostle John declares, "for whom the Son sets free is free indeed."

CHAPTER 9

WRITE THE VISION

"…The greatest song has yet to be sung, who will sing it?
The greatest book has yet to be written, who will write it?
The greatest melody has yet to be played, who will play it?
The greatest portrait has yet to be painted, who will paint it …?
—Michael S. Nimmons Commencement Speech, Breslin
Student Events Center, Michigan State University, Fall 98'

Dec of 1998, I graduated from Michigan State University
with my Bachelors in Political Theory and Constitutional
Democracy. It was a very special day in my life for a number
of different reasons, I was the first in my family to graduate
from college, so there was a definite sense of pride from not
just myself but from my family as they made the trek up to
East Lansing for my Commencement Ceremonies. But, one
very important reason it was a special day for me was because
I was going to be the Morning "Class Speaker" for the entire
Fall Graduating class of 1998. I would have the opportunity
to give this address at the Breslin Student Events Center;
where the Michigan State Spartans Basketball Team play.

This milestone moment in my young life made graduating from college all the more special.

The Influence of King

As it turns out, public speaking and oratory was a passion of mine ever since I was a very young boy. I can recall being introduced to Dr. Martin Luther King Jr. by my father after watching the "King" min-series on TV. My dad had several albums of Dr. King's speeches and I remembered listening to them and being completely mesmerized by his deep baritone voice, and being enamored with his oratory and command of the English language. In Dr. King's speeches, they reflected a well-read intellectual, who was an expert at incorporating his literary prose into his sermons and public addresses. I remember as a kid listening almost every day to the Dr. King albums my dad had and trying to emulate his speech pattern, and his baritone voice. In fact, I listened so much that I mastered it almost down to his exact enunciation of every word. I would begin reciting speeches like "I've Been to the Mountaintop" and "I Have a Dream" at my church and school assemblies. I even had an opportunity to deliver a Dr. King speech during the Annual Dr. King weekend celebration in Detroit at Cobo Hall. Public speaking has always been a passion of mine, and Dr. King was truly one of my major adolescent influences.

I not only enjoyed listening to Dr. King's speeches, but I also enjoyed reading his speeches as well. In fact, reading his speeches begin to open up my paradigm to other speakers, and authors of like mind and passion. I wanted to know where certain passages and phrases came from that he quoted in some of his most famous speeches, and all of this open up a new world to me. And, what this immense study into the life of Dr. King begin to show me was that I too can become as powerful a speaker as he was, I too can possess the talent and the skill to write as well as l deliver powerful speeches about a variety of different subject matter. Subsequently, in high school I was entered into oratorical contests by my teachers and counselors; who recognized my natural speaking ability. The Detroit Public Schools had an Arts & Literary Dept. and they often conducted Oratorical Contests where students from highs schools across the city could compete and win monetary prizes. The first oratorical contest that I participated in was entitled "Do Minorities Need a Revolution of The Mind?" The contest had two tiers of competition to it, the first one was to give your speech to a panel of judges down at the Detroit Board of Education Building on Woodward Ave. I remember working extremely hard on not just writing the speech but delivering it, and what I also did to help myself stand out more amongst the other students who were competing was to memorize the entire speech. From birth, I was blessed with the ability to memorize anything fairly quickly, and so once I completed the speech I begin to commit it to memory so that I could not only impress the judges with words, but with my delivery as well. Walking into a room for an audition, and you have no notes, folders or whatsoever to distract you to the judges is extremely impressive. Especially to a panel of judges who are used to seeing students walk in with notes and other materials to speak from. So, I walked in and introduced myself and begin my presentation and I could tell by some of the expressions on the judges faces that their minds were completely blown. Here is an articulate, intelligent, young man from Mumford High School speaking like he's been doing this professionally for years. Needless to say, I advanced to the second and final round where the finalist was invited to the Charles Wright African American Museum, where they would compete for a $1000 savings bond. I remember how nervous I was, this being the first time I would actually speak competitively and yet there was a calming presence that I felt, ensuring me that all of my weeks preparation and labor was not going to be in vain. As I sat and watched the other finalist give their speeches I took mental notes on the do's and don'ts of public speaking. I recall one such contestant who instead of speaking at the lectern, which was set up at the front of the room to speak from where the judges and the audience could clearly see him, he decided to speak from the floor with this back to the audience; only speaking to the judges. As I sat there and watched him turn his body towards the judges and completely alienate the audience, I could see from some of the judges faces that he had loss the competition. That was definitely not something that I was going to do. When I got up to deliver my prepared speech, I remember mentally becoming "King." I took on his mannerism, his baritone voice but this time it was my words. I remember delivering that speech with so much power that when I finished every member of the intimate audience wanted to clap but because they were instructed not to, respectfully tried to constrain their emotions. When the judges returned from their deliberations, I was excited to find that I had won 1st Place in my first oratorical competition, which would lead to several more prize-winning speeches and great opportunities to exercise my god given talent. Competing in oratorical contest actually became a great way for me to network as well as hone my speaking ability skills. Even when I matriculated to Michigan State University I continued my speaking career there while a student on this massive campus. I competed in one of Operation PUSH's Oratorical Contested hosted by Judge Greg Mathis, where I won a $5000 scholarship. The theme for this competition was "Education Today, Shaping Our Communities Tomorrow."

You Got to Start Somewhere

The Bible teaches is Zechariah 4:10 "Do not despise small beginnings ..." You have to start somewhere; your journey has to begin somewhere; and one things for sure if you ever plan to excel to a greater and even higher level, one thing remains true, you have to start somewhere. It's at the beginning where you learn you toughest and greatest lessons. It's from the beginning that we are a little rough around the edges, it's from the beginning that things may not be as smooth as you like. But, if you continue; which you have to do as well, you will get to the place that God wants you to be.

The important thing that I learned early on in my speaking career is you have to start somewhere. No one ever starts on the top of the mountain, but they have to start out making the climb of the mountain and yes it will be some treacherous moments during your climb, yes it will be sometimes where you may not want to go any further, but if you ever want to reach the top you got to start somewhere. As much as I am writing this advice to you who are reading this chapter I am also writing it to myself. There is probably no one more impatient than I am when it comes to seeing the progress from a time that has been well invested. I better than anyone understand that our destinies have been divinely carved out by our Creator and He ultimately holds the timing of purpose in his hands. But, I find myself wanting it to happen sooner rather than later and sometimes I let my impatience get the best of me which is something you can't do when walking with God. You have to trust that He knows what He's doing and wait for Him to set your life in its proper order. Although it is our natural inclination to try to hurry God or get ahead of Him, because either you feel His plan is taking too long or you have a better plan altogether. However, we must understand that vision must be accompanied by patience, because while you are waiting for it to come to pass God is working on you during the process. The problem is we don't understand that we are not ready to get what God has for us in the time that we want it to happen. And this is why God delays the process a bit until we get to where He wants us to be. So, a word of advice, if it hasn't happened yet, or if isn't happening fast enough that might be an indication there is still worked to be done on ourselves. We; however, tend to look to query God about the nature of the delay, but His response is always, "you're not waiting on me, I'm waiting on you." In His time, you are everything He created you to be; in His time, you are well into fulfilling your purpose. Never be afraid to examine yourself; never be afraid to look at yourself introspectively. Remember *"the unexamined life is a life not worth living."* Never be afraid to look yourself in the mirror. This is why we said in the previous chapter that fulfilling a vision is as much about you discovering yourself as it is realizing a lifelong dream or goal. There is still much about yourself that you don't know, there is still some growing that you have to do. This is why it is important that we are honest with ourselves throughout the process. Our parents often told us, "honesty is the best policy." And we appreciated this advice when we were young and our parents wanted to know who ate the last slice of pizza or did you do your homework. But, as we got older something changed. It's not that we stop continuing to be honest, but instead we redirected that honesty externally instead of where it is needed the most-internally. As we got older the less honest we were with ourselves. We overestimate our strengths and underestimate our weaknesses, which end up giving us an inaccurate picture of ourselves. God is the only one that knows us better than we know ourselves, and that is why it's important that we trust Him over one another. We tend to think that we should be much further along than we actually are, which may mean that we actually need more work than we believe is necessary to get to where we need to go. The reality is we are always somewhere in the middle when it comes to where we are and where we are supposed to be.

The Tool of Oratory

Competing in oratorical contests was extremely invigorating, the idea of writing an original speech from a topic that was given really put me in a real positive space. I liked these types of contests for a number of reasons; for one I really felt important, because being able to put my thoughts and beliefs into a speech that will be heard by other people and will be given serious consideration. I also felt a spiritual connection with the likes of such men as Thurgood Marshall, Frederick Douglas, W.E.B. Dubois, Dr. King and other black intellectuals who used this tool of oratory to craft some of their greatest and most impactful speeches. My speaking career begin to take off at very young age. In addition, to speaking during these contests, I was speaking at churches and for community organizations and for banquets and dinners. Every opportunity I was given to stand before an audience I wanted to take full advantage of it. I was taught visualization at an early age and even while I was rehearsing and practicing my speeches for oratorical contests, keynotes, etc., I would be envisioning the audience captivated by our linguistic presentation. Each time I would visualize an audience, it would be large and vast and we would leave them spellbound by our oratory. This visual exercise helped to build our confidence to speak in front of audiences large and small. Even during those times where we were in front of an audience that might not be what we had prepared for, while we were yet speaking we would engage in visualization that helped us to continue speaking as if it was the crowd we had prepared for. And as our confidence continued to build God would put us in front of the crowds that we visualized in our mind, and we soaked up every moment, every opportunity to share in the gift that we believe God gave us. We believe God would periodically give us a foretaste of things to come as long as we continued in the path that He laid out for us to follow. Each opportunity we wanted to build towards the next one, always trying to capitalize on the moment that God had given us. With each speech, with each oratorical contest, with each award, we felt like we were building towards something. A culminating moment on the grandest of stages that would catapult us into the next level of our perceived calling. So, when I discovered there was an opportunity to be the Class Speaker at my own graduation, I begin doing my research to find out what the process entails and how I could be apart. I saw this as a unique opportunity to make graduation a day that I will never forget. For me, vision was setting small goals that will eventually lead to bigger and greater goals that will eventually put you right where you want to be. I appropriately titled my commencement address, "Write the Vision, And Make It Plain." This was a scriptural reference from Habakkuk 2:2 where God is giving the prophet Habakkuk specific instructions regarding the vision that he was given by God, and how this vision should be disseminated to His people. The speech and my vision were uniquely intertwined because my vision-at the time, was to speak at my graduation and the theme of my speech was about vision.

I remember writing it and committing it to memory, rehearsing it in my off-campus apartment every chance that I got. Envisioning in my mind the moment, the opportunity where I would walk into my divine purpose. When the time came to go before the auditioning panel for class speakers for Fall Commencement, I felt like I was more than prepared for this opportunity. Keeping in mind, my entire life; it seemed had been building towards this moment. Once there I introduced myself, paused for a brief moment and immediately went right into my prepared speech. I had no notes in front of me, so the panel had no idea what I was going to do or say, because there was nothing in front of me to indicate what I would be doing next. I had committed the speech to memory, which is always a plus in situations like these, because it serves as automatic bonus over those who are relegated to their notes. It instantly demonstrates the level of preparation that you have given in order to get to this point. And, so I delivered my speech with the poise and grace of Dr. King, and the vernacular and presence of a college professor. When I was done, I truly felt I had given it my best and the only thing left was to wait to be notified by the committee if I had made the final cut of speakers for graduation.

A short time passed, and I remember opening the letter that I received from the class speaker's committee notifying me of the results of our audition. And, when I read the letter I was overwhelmed to find that I would be the class speaker for my graduation from Michigan State University. And, this speech would be given at the Breslin Student Events Center where the Men's Spartan Basketball Team plays with a seating capacity of close to 17,000. I remember the day of graduation, where my family and few of my close friends came up from Detroit to wish us well. My pastor- Dr. Charles Ellis; at the time, and his wife First Lady Crisette came up to show their support. It definitely was a special occasion that I will not soon forget. I remember marching in with the distinguish dais of School Administrators, the President of MSU M. Peter McPherson, the Board of Directors, Deans and other distinguished guests. I was seated right next to the President of the Board of Directors for the entire university. It looked like from the stage the stadium was filled to capacity, and I could feel a few butterflies beginning to settle in. But, I reflected back on the time of preparation that I had lead up to this point. Not just the time that it took preparing to deliver this speech, but the many speeches before this that help to build and shape me into the speaker that I was. I remember very vividly the moment when President M. Peter McPherson introduced us and we walk to the podium and after a brief pause when begin to deliver the speech that we had been waiting our whole life to deliver. I remember it like it was yesterday, we begin by saying,

"We stand here on this 12th day of December 1998 adding yet another chapter to our history book. Each of us has a separate book in which we continue adding pages on an almost regular

basis. Our first words, our first steps, our first jobs, our proms and high school graduations and now another chapter is being added to the book that we have written … Every great man who has ever become great first became great because of vision. The first model "T" was envisioned inside the head of a dreamer. A simple process involving four wheels and an engine has now become one man's primary means of transportation. Our nation which was founded on the principles of liberty and justice. Principles that were first espoused in our nation's most treasured transcript of independence. Thomas Jefferson openly declared that, "We hold these truths to be self-evident that all men are created equal that they are endowed by their Creator, with such inalienable rights as life, liberty and the pursuit of happiness … And so today as we matriculate from here to our appointed destinations this is not a fairy tale of sorts. We haven't envisioned this day in our minds only to occupy time and another person's money. But this is an investment into a future that is sure to bring prosperous dividends … All of which had to had been birth by a vision. A vision that is not satisfied until it runs its course, a vision that isn't effective until it accomplished everything that it has set out to do …"

We even quoted Shakespeare's "Hamlet" in this magnum opus of speeches we delivered for this special day. We concluded with a compelling charge to all of the imminent graduates of this great university to,

"…embrace our one moment in time and use this time as it was intended. The vision that you glorify in your mind, the ideal that you enthrone in your heart, this you will build your life by this you will become."

When we were done delivering this speech, we received; according to the President of the MSU Board of Directors, the first ever standing ovation that a class speaker had ever been given. It truly was a day to remember, and whether or not this was the culminating moment that God had been preparing us for, the mantra that we chose to live by is to approach every opportunity as if it were your last. In essence, every opportunity deserves your best, every audience deserves the best of you, every stage deserves your best performance. You should never short change your audience, because of their size, enthusiasm, energy or the like.

I shared this moment with you, because it was one of the pivotal reasons that I decided to write this book. Just as I chose vision as the theme of my speech, I chose vision as the theme of this book, because like you, I am not done dreaming, I'm not done seeing the potential that lies in tomorrow. I too, have big dreams, big visions, and big goals that I'm still in pursuit of. This book is in no way an expert guide on how to fulfill your dream or vision. Instead it is a commentary on the brilliance of vision, the ebullience of vision that causes us to a see a brighter future even when our present day is cluttered with grey clouds.

As we conclude this book we want to leave you with some practical points that can help you as you continue to map out and strategize the dreams and visions that you have yet to achieve. Again, the advice that we offer in this book is only to help to empower and inspire you to live out your dreams. We are still yet in the middle of the process, so as much as we are writing to others we are also writing this book for ourselves.

Write it Down

One of the very important things to do as you begin to map out your vision and dreams that you desire to achieve, take some time to write them down. Your mind should never be the only place where vision and dreams reside. Take time to write them down on paper, put them on a vision board or a goal board so that you can see them every day that you wake up in the morning. Once you have them written down you now have established a written contract between yourself and your future that you will not let these ideas go unfulfilled. Believe it or not, the effort that it takes to write them down on paper or post them on a vision or goal board means they are now officially apart of your daily routine. They are officially apart of your natural, mental and spiritual regiment. You are not only thinking about them, but you are seeing them every day, and you are not only seeing them but you are now praying and asking God for the direction to bring these things to pass. It is so very important that you do this, because as long as they remain solely in your subconscious or conscious mind then they tend to be approached casually; you're only thinking about it when you have time, you may give it some thought periodically. And, subconsciously you are telling yourself that this may or may not happened. So, when these implicit messages is floating through your mental skies then your treat your vision and dreams as such, daydreams to just occupy the time; superficial dreams that you have subconsciously convinced yourself will never happen. The question then becomes, why think about them? Whey entertain them? Why allow them to take up space in your mind, if you are not serious about pursuing them? Once you have sorted through the answers to these questions and realized that your dreams are far too important to approach casually, but they make up the future that I see for myself. Thomas Edison spoke of this very thing very pointedly, "vision without execution is hallucination." So, you have to decide today that you are not going to allow your dreams to amount to mere hallucinations, and continue in the doldrums and cynical machinations that you call your life, but you are going to approach your dreams with all of the drive, tenacity, and fervor y that you can muster. And, the very first step in this process is to write them down. Writing them down now makes you officially accountable for what you see, it now puts your vision and dreams front and center in the forefront of your mind. And, every waking moment you are strategizing and thinking about how you can; with the help of the Lord, bring them to pass. Writing them down is also your sign to God that you are serious about the future He has given you to pursue. Once He sees that you are serious about the vision He's given you then He'll begin to lead you and guide down the path to bringing them from concept to reality. Remember God never gives you a vision without provision. So, He's already secured the provision for you, as we said earlier, God is just waiting on us. The question is, are you ready to pursue your dreams; are you ready to pursue your vision; are you ready to be better; are you ready to be more; are you ready for your future? If the answer is yes to all these questions, then the hardest part of this journey has already been completed.

The Right People v. The Wrong People

One of the next important things to do in this journey of fulfillment is to find you a mentor or a role model that you can shadow and observe. And, whether your mentor is someone that you know personally and they have consented to take you under their wing and show you what they did to help you strategize your vision, or your mentor or role model is someone that you can only observe from a far. Maybe they are a celebrity or television personality or public figure that you don't have direct access to. But, instead you can follow their story, read about their humble beginnings, use their story as inspiration for your own. It is important that you surround yourself around positive people that you can help to motivate and influence you to pursue your dreams.

Relationships like these are important to have, but it is also very important to have the right people in your company. It's one thing to know people, but it's another thing entirely to know the right people. And, as I get older and more mature, the more important it is to know the right people, and to have the right people in your company. The right people are those who you can share secrets with, who you can be transparent with, who you can share your fears and anxieties with and they won't judge you, they won't persecute you. Instead, they will pray with you and for you, they will encourage and motivate you. I'm grateful to have the right people within my own circle of friends. There are a group of guys that I graduated from Michigan State University with and we call ourselves "The Five Heartbeats." The name came from one of our favorite movies we watched while students on Michigan State's campus. These guys are a collection of positive brothers that I know and we inspire one another. We get together for breakfast every other month and talk about what we're doing and collaborate and empower one another's dreams and visions. They are a group of guys that individually are doing some great things and collectively we can do even greater things. I value their friendship and counsel, and I am godly proud of each of them and thankful that He put them in my life.

Having the right people in your life is a great thing, but having the wrong people in your life can be very costly to your vision and dreams. The right people help you, the wrong people will hurt you. The right people inspire and encourage you, the wrong people antagonize and criticize you. This is why it so important you that you thoroughly vet the people that you bring into your circle of influence. By vetting; I mean, pray about them, observe them, watch them, ask God for discernment when considering whether they are the right fit for you to bring into your company. This vetting process is for your peace of mind, you have to be careful who you are transparent with. You have to be careful who chose to be vulnerable with, because the right people will cover you, the wrong people will expose you. And, when it comes to sharing your vision you should definitely be very selective on who are confide in and who you chose to share the secrets of your heart with. Joseph's own brothers conspired to kill him after he told them of the vision that God gave him that they would bow down and worship him. Everyone is not able to handle your success; everyone is not able to handle your potential. In fact, everyone should not be given the opportunity to do either one. This is why you have to be very selective and prayerful when looking for like-minded people to link up with as you embark upon this journey of fulfillment.

Read, Read, Read

Another thing that is very important to do during this journey of fulfillment in addition to surrounding yourself around the "right" people is to find ways to internalize as much positivity and inspiration as possible. There is no better way of doing this than to carve out time daily to read. When you are not able to personally link up with a mentor or role model to help guide you through this journey of fulfillment, you can certainly read their life story. Read about their successes and failures; read about the pitfalls to watch out for. Internalize the advice they provide within the pages of their life story. I personally have challenged myself this year to read 1 book per month, and so far, I have stayed on track with my reading and I'm finding myself more inspired, more intellectually inquisitive; in other words, the more I read the more I want to read, the more I know the more that I want to know. In this quest for fulfillment, knowledge should be your closest companion. The more you know the better equipped you are for the journey ahead. There is nothing more relaxing and intellectually rewarding than taking time to read a book. I personally feel I watch entirely too much television and if I'm not watching television than I'm surfing the web looking at the various social media platforms that I'm a part of. I am constantly trying to influence my children to do the same. Growing up in this technologically advanced society; where everything is literally at your fingertips, it has made us lazy and complacent. If we can't have it now, then we don't want it. If the activity takes time away from us doing what we want to do now, then we don't want to do it. Over time the value of reading has diminished. But, we have to redirect that, we have reintroduced that to this generation of young people. So, taking time away from those technological hindrances, won't kill us, it won't harm us, instead it gives us more time to exercise our brain power, it gives us more time to exercise our intellectual muscles by simply taking the time to read a book.

While reading your life can be inspired by someone else's life, your vision can become clearer by seeing someone else's vision. We cannot discount the age-old art of reading. Read everything that you can get your hands on that relates to the dreams and visions that you would like to pursue. Again, no one is going to be more vested into your vision than you are, so take the time to invest into your vision, because the more you invest into your vision the more you are investing into yourself. There is no one more valuable than you are, no one worthier of your time than you are. Why not take the time to invest into your future, invest into yourself by finding things to do that will empower you, inspire you, motivate you to continue to pursue your dreams?

Just Do It

And, finally there is nothing more important in all the advice we've given in this book that you need to take with you on this journey of fulfillment than the admonishment to "Just Do It." This is a very familiar slogan from the Nike Corporation that is easily the most recognizable slogan in the world. While it is the most recognizable slogan in probably the world, there is probably no truer statement that has ever been uttered. This concluding chapter of this book is designed to literally be a call to action. Once you have read the first eight chapters, this final concluding chapter is essentially asking, what you are going to do next? After reading and internalizing the godly wisdom and advice we have shared about vision and our thoughts on how important it is to pursue your vision and dreams, this chapter has been strategically designed to give you the shot in the arm you need to get started.

What are you going to do next? What is your next move? What are you going to do make the world a better place to live in? What are you going to do about world hunger? What are you going to do about the plight of today's youth? What you are going to do about climate change? What will be the next innovation? These are all questions that you will eventually help to answer. I believe that you are the person reading this book that has the cure for cancer. I believe that the person reading this book has the cure for the AIDS epidemic. I believe that the person reading this book has the intellect and the knowledge to be the next President of the United States. I believe that the person reading this book has the athletic ability and basketball acumen to be the next Lebron James or Steph Curry. I believe that the person reading this book has the brain power to be the next Nobel Peace Prize winner. I believe the person reading this book has the power to change the world.

My expectations for you are tremendous, my expectations for the youth reading this book is that they will be the next leaders of this country and the world, my expectations for the adults reading this book is that they will become the role models and mentors that are young people need to achieve their dreams. My expectations for the people reading this book are limitless. I want to speak directly to every person reading this book that you matter, your vision matters, your dreams matter, your life matters. You are only limited by your thinking, you can be whatever you want to be, you can do whatever you set your mind to do you. Don't let anyone discourage you or diminish your desire to dream. Henry David Thoreau said, "Go confidently in the direction of your dreams. Live the life that you've imagined." Not truer words have ever been uttered. You too have to believe in your dreams when no one else will, believe in yourself when no one else will. Just do it is probably the most valuable advice you will get from this book. You are the one that is going to make it happen; you are the person the world is looking to for answers, you are the one that will be the next inventor, you are the one that will be next Pulitzer Prize winner, you will be the next Head of State, you will be the next Academy Award winner. The success of your vision hinges on the decisions that you will make. The success of your dreams is tied to the choices that you decide to make. You have what it takes, the potential already rests within you. There is no one the world needs more than you; the world needs your genius, the world needs your brilliance, the world needs your ideas, the world needs your intelligence. The question is will you the be the one, or will it be someone else. Will you be the one that cures cancer, or will it be someone else? Will you be the one that brokers peace around the globe, or will it be someone else?

Who's Next?

The history books are filled with successful people; people that the world should forever thank for their intellect, their genius, their individual contribution to the well-being of the entire world. There are so many people that have already accomplished so much and contributed so much to the advancement of our society. The only question that remains, is who's next? In fact, we spend a lot of time rehearsing the accomplishments of the past, we spend a lot of time talking about the Albert Einstein's, and the Alexander Graham Bell's, the Garret Morris's and the Thomas Edison's. Yes, a lot of time is spent talking about the accomplishments of the Fannie Lou Hamer's, and the Harriet Tubman's and Sojourner Truth's. We spend a great deal of time talking about the achievements of John F. Kennedy, Theodore Roosevelt, Franklin D. Roosevelt. A number of books have been written about the William Jefferson Clinton's, the Thurgood Marshall's, the W.E.B. Dubois and the Barack Obama's. History has well recorded their successes and failures; history has a record of their crowning achievements. The question that still remains, is who's next?

So much focus, many times is put on those who've already cross the threshold of success that we almost seem to be a people that are preoccupied with the past. What was done, what was achieved, what was discovered? But, rarely if ever do we entertain the question of who's next? The implication is always there, but rarely do we address it, rarely do we focus our undivided attention on the merits of this question. Why is that? Is it because, we don't know who's next until someone inevitably steps forward? There may be something to this, because history is only able to record the accomplishments of those who dare to step out from the shadows of obscurity into the bright light of the future; history is only able to record the successes of those men who don't; according to George Bernard Shaw, "see things as they are and ask, Why? I see things that never were and ask, Why not?" The future is only as promising as you see it, which is why you have to look with eyes of optimism and not ones of fear.

One of the most innovative inventors in African American History-George Washington Carver asserted, "where there is no vision there is no hope." Echoing the words of the wisest King to ever walk the face of the earth, in Proverbs 29:18, (KJV) King Solomon declared, "where there is no vision the people perish ..." Implicit within this statement from King Solomon is the reality that death accompanies those who have no vision. One of the primary symptoms of hopelessness is lack of vision, lack of direction. Our lives must be consumed by vision. Vision must be the reason we get out of the bed in the morning, and the anticipation of it is the reason we go to bed at night. Leaders have to lead with vision, in the same way Warren Bennis instructs, "leadership is the capacity to translate vision into reality." My question is the same as the interlocutors of John the Baptist; who were sent by John to ask of Jesus one of the most theologically penetrating and compelling questions of our time, "are you the one or should be look for another?" This is question that I pose to each and every reader of this book, are you the one that will take this world further than it is haver been, are you the one that will see what has never been seen, are you the one that will travel to heights unknown? At the end of the day, the only one that truly knows the answer to this question is also the only person the responsibility of your tomorrow fully rests upon, and that person is YOU! You are both the question and the answer, you are both the problem and the solution, the cause and the cure, the period and the comma. You are the centerpiece of this experiment called life, and what you make of it is entirely up to you. So, if the world is waiting on you, then what are you waiting on, if the future is waiting on you, then what are you waiting on, if tomorrow is waiting on you, then what are you waiting on? You are the reason we wrote this book, you are the person we've been speaking to in every chapter and verse of this text. Your significance is beyond measure, your value is tremendous, your worth is beyond compare. From this day forth vow to yourself that you will strive everyday to live it to the fullest, live everyday as if it were your last. So, when it's all said and done and your final breath has been released the world will collectively thank God for your existence as it pays tribute to a life well lived and a vision fulfilled.

REFERENCES

1. Barack Obama speech to joint session of Congress, September 2009. (2017, August 21). Retrieved September 01, 2017, from https://en.m.wikipedia. org/wiki/Barack_Obama_speech_to_joint_ session_of_Congress,_September_2009
2. Munroe, M. (2003). *The Principles and Power of Vision*. New Kensington, PA: Whitaker House.
3. Carroll, Lewis, Chapter 6, "Pig & Pepper". (1981). In *Alice Adventures in Wonderland & Through the Looking Glass* (pp. 42-53). New York, NY: Bantam Dell.
4. Les Brown Quote. (n.d.). Retrieved September 01, 2017, from http://www.azquotes.com/quote/1316041
5. Donne, J. (1987). *Devotions Upon Emergent Occasions*. New York, NY: Oxford University Press, Inc.
6. Henry David Thoreau Quotes. (n.d.). Retrieved September 01, 2017, from https://www.brainyquote. com/quotes/quotes/h/henrydavid163028.html
7. King, M. L., Jr. (1986). "I See The Promised land". In *I Have a Dream; Writing and Speeches that Changed the World* (Ist ed., pp. 193-203). New York, NY: HarperSanFrancisco.

8. Shadyac, T. (Director). (2003, May 23). *"Bruce Almighty"* [Video file]. Retrieved, September 1, 2017, from http://www.imdb.com/title/tt0315327/

9. King, M. L., Jr, & Moss, O., Jr. (1998). "A Knock at Midnight". In *A Knock at Midnight* (pp. 61-78). New York, NY: Warner Books.

10. Shakespeare, W. (n.d.). Act 1, Scene 3 "A Room in Pololnious House". In *Hamlet (AmazonClassics Edition) (Paperback* (pp. 25-30). Seattle: AmazonClassic.

11. YOU CAN'T HURRY GOD Lyrics - CHICAGO MASS CHOIR. (n.d.). Retrieved September 01, 2017, from http://www.elyrics.net/read/c/chicago-mass-choir-lyrics/you-can t-hurry-god-lyrics.html

12. A quote by Michelangelo Buonarroti. (n.d.). Retrieved September 01, 2017, from https://www.goodreads.com/quotes/557979-the-greatest-danger-for-most-of-us-is-not-that

13. Henley, W. E., & Henley, W. E. (1900). *For Englands sake, verses and songs in time of war.* London: D. Nutt.

14. Page, M. (2014, October 14). Tribute to Detroit Renaissance High School Student Billy Watts: Life and Death played out on Social Media. Retrieved September 01, 2017, from http://www.marlinpage.com/2014/tribute-to-detroit-renaissance-high-school-student-billy-watts-life-and-death-played-out-on-social-media/

15. When there is no enemy within, the enemies outside cannot hurt you. (n.d.). Retrieved September 01, 2017, from https://tinybuddha.com/wisdom-quotes/when-there-is-no-enemy-within-the-enemies-outside-cannot-hurt-you-2/
AFRICAN PROVERB

16. Blaszczak-Boxe, A. (2014, June 25). Watching too much TV could shorten your life. Retrieved September 01, 2017, from https://www.cbsnews.com/news/watching-too-much-tv-could-shorten-your-life/

17. A quote from The Fountainhead. (n.d.). Retrieved September 01, 2017, from https://www.goodreads.com/quotes/310800-throughout-the-centuries-there-were-men-who-took-first-steps

18. Keller, H. (n.d.). Helen Keller Quotes. Retrieved September 01, 2017, from https://www.brainyquote.com/quotes/quotes/h/helenkelle383771.html

19. 2014 Rose Bowl. (2017, July 02). Retrieved September 01, 2017, from https://en.wikipedia.org/wiki/2014_Rose_Bowl

20. Mandela, N. (2013, December 12). Action without vision is only passing time, vision without action is merely day dreaming, but vision with action can change the world. Retrieved September 01, 2017, from http://philosiblog.com/2013/12/12/action-without-vision-is-only-passing-time-vision-without-action-is-merely-day-dreaming-but-vision-with-action-can-change-the-world/

21. Nelson Mandela. (2017, August 28). Retrieved September 01, 2017, from https://en.wikipedia.org/wiki/Nelson_Mandela

22. Tubman, H. (2016, April 21). Harriet Tubman: 'I Freed a Thousand Slaves'. Retrieved September 01, 2017, from http://www.snopes.com/harriet-tubman-quote/

23. X, M. (1963, January 23). "Malcolm describes the difference between the 'house Negro' and the 'field Negro.'". Retrieved September 01, 2017, from http://ccnmtl.columbia.edu/projects/mmt/mxp/speeches/mxa17.html

Brown, Les. Les Brown Quotes (Author of Living Your Dreams) Retrieved September 13, 2017

24. https://www.goodreads.com/author/quotes/57803. Les Brow

25. US, T. C. (2016, October 11). What it means to be black in the American educational system. Retrieved September 01, 2017, from http://www.huffingtonpost.com/the-conversation-us/what-it-means-to-be-black_b_12442448.html

26. Shaw, G. B. (1949). Respectfully Quoted, A Dictionary of Quotations. Retrieved September 01, 2017, from http://www.bartleby.com/73/465.html

27. Bennis, W. (1989). Leader Power That No One Has. In *Why Leaders Can't Lead* (pp. 142-147). Los Angeles, CA: University of Southern California.

Printed in the United States
By Bookmasters